George F. Trayes

Five Months on a German Raider

weitsuechtig

George F. Trayes

Five Months on a German Raider

ISBN/EAN: 9783956560231

Auflage: 1

Erscheinungsjahr: 2013

Erscheinungsort: Bremen, Deutschland

@ weitsuechtig in Access Verlag GmbH. Alle Rechte beim Verlag und bei den jeweiligen Lizenzgebern.

weitsuechtig

The author before and after his five months captivity

DEDICATED

IN DEEP GRATITUDE TO THE DANISH NAVAL AU-
THORITIES,
LIGHTHOUSE KEEPERS, LIFEBOATMEN AND THEIR FAMI-
LIES,
AND THE KINDLY INHABITANTS OF SKAGEN, DENMARK,
WHO SECURED FOR US, AND WELCOMED US BACK
TO FREEDOM, AND WHO BY THEIR OVERWHELMING
KINDNESS AND HEARTY HELP
AND HOSPITALITY LEFT WITH US SUCH
KIND AND HAPPY MEMORIES
OF THEIR COUNTRY AND
COUNTRYMEN AS
WILL NEVER BE
FORGOTTEN.

Contents

Chapter I. The Capture of the "Hitachi Maru"	1
Chapter II. Prisoners on the „Wolf"	8
Chapter III. Back to the „Hitachi Maru"	16
Chapter IV. The Germans Sink Their Prize	24
Chapter V. Life on the „Wolf"	33
Chapter VI. Another Prize – Our Future Home	42
Chapter VII. Christmas on the „Igotz Mendi"	50
Chapter VIII. Rumours and Plans	61
Chapter IX – En Route for Ruhleben – Via Iceland	70
Chapter X. Saved by Shipwreck	79
Chapter XI. Free at Last	89

Illustrations

The author before and after his five months captivity	front page
„Hitachi" passengers and crew in lifeboats after their ship had been shelled. From an enlargement of photo taken on the Wolf by a German officer.	7
Nippon Yusen Kaisha S.S. „Hitachi Maru".	31
The "Igotz Mendi" ashore at Skagen. Taken on the morning of our rescue.	80
The Skagen lifeboat going out to the "Igotz Mendi" to bring off the prisoners.	90
The Skagen lifeboat bringing tosShore the prisoners from the „Igotz Mendi".	90
At Skagen: German prizec rew of the" Igotz Mendi" under guard, awaiting internment.	98
Map showing track oft her raider „Wolf"	102

Chapter I. The Capture of the "Hitachi Maru"

The S.S. *Hitachi Maru*, 6,716 tons, of the Nippon Yushen Kaisha (Japan Mail Steamship Co.), left Colombo on September 24, 1917, her entire ship's company being Japanese. Once outside the breakwater, the rough weather made itself felt; the ship rolled a good deal and the storms of wind and heavy rain continued more or less all day. The next day the weather had moderated, and on the succeeding day, Wednesday, the 26th, fine and bright weather prevailed, but the storm had left behind a long rolling swell.

My wife and I were bound for Cape Town, and had joined the ship at Singapore on the 15th, having left Bangkok, the capital of Siam, a week earlier. Passengers who had embarked at Colombo were beginning to recover from their sea-sickness and had begun to indulge in deck games, and there seemed every prospect of a pleasant and undisturbed voyage to Delagoa Bay, where we were due on October 7th.

The chart at noon on the 26th marked 508 miles from Colombo, 2,912 to Delagoa Bay, and 190 to the Equator; only position, not the course, being marked after the ship left Colombo. Most of the passengers had, as usual, either dozed on deck or in their cabins after tiffin, my wife and I being in deck chairs on the port side. When I woke up at 1.45 I saw far off on the horizon, on the port bow, smoke from a steamer. I was the only person awake on the deck at the time, and I believe no other passenger had seen the smoke, which was so far away that it was impossible to tell whether we were meeting or overtaking the ship.

Immediately thoughts of a raider sprang to my mind, though I did not know one was out. But from what one could gather at Colombo, no ship was due at that port on that track in about two days. The streets of Colombo were certainly darkened at night, and the lighthouse was not in use when we were there, but there was no mention of the presence of any suspicious craft in the adjacent waters.

It is generally understood that instructions to Captains in these times are to suspect every vessel seen at sea, and to run away from all signs of smoke (and some of us knew that on a previous occasion, some months before, a vessel of the same line had seen smoke in this neighbourhood, and had at once turned tail and made tracks for Colombo, resuming her voyage when the smoke disappeared). The officer on the bridge with his glass must have seen the smoke long before I did, so my suspicions of a raider were gradually disarmed as we did not alter our course a single point, but proceeded to meet the stranger, whose course towards us formed a diagonal one with ours. If nothing had happened she would have crossed our track slightly astern of us.

But something did happen. More passengers were now awake, discussing the nationality of the ship bearing down on us. Still no alteration was made in our course, and we and she had made no sign of recognition.

Surely everything was all right and there was nothing to fear. Even the Japanese commander of the gun crew betrayed no anxiety on the matter, but stood with the passengers on the deck watching the oncoming stranger. Five bells had just gone when the vessel, then about seven hundred yards away from us, took a sudden turn to port and ran up signals and the German Imperial Navy flag. There was no longer any doubt—the worst had happened. We had walked blindly into the open arms of the enemy. The signals were to tell us to stop. We did not stop. The raider fired two shots across our bows, and they fell into the sea quite close to where most of the passengers were standing. Still we did not stop. It was wicked to ignore these orders and warnings, as there was no possible chance of escape from an armed vessel of any kind. The attempt to escape had been left too late; it should have been made immediately the smoke of the raider was seen. Most of the passengers went to their cabins for life-belts and life-saving waistcoats, and at once returned to the deck to watch the raider. As we were still steaming and had not even yet obeyed the order to stop, the raider opened fire on us in dead earnest, firing a broadside.

While the firing was going on, a seaplane appeared above the raider; some assert that she dropped bombs in front of us, but personally I did not see this.

The greatest alarm now prevailed on our ship, and passengers did not know where to go to avoid the shells which we could hear and feel striking the ship. My wife and I returned to our cabin to fetch an extra pair of spectacles, our passports, and my pocketbook, and at the same time picked up her jewel-case. The alley-way between the companion-way and our cabin was by this time strewn with splinters of wood and glass and wreckage; pieces of shell had been embedded in the panelling and a large hole made in the funnel. This damage had been done by a single shot aimed at the wireless room near the bridge.

We returned once more to the port deck, where most of the first-class passengers had assembled waiting for orders — which never came. No instructions came from the Captain or officers or crew; in fact, we never saw any of the ship's officers until long after all the lifeboats were afloat on the sea.

The ship had now stopped, and the firing had apparently ceased, but we did not know whether it would recommence, and of course imagined the Germans were firing to sink the ship. It was useless trying to escape the shots, as we did not then know at what part of the ship the Germans were firing, so there was only one thing for the passengers to do — to leave the ship as rapidly as possible, as we all thought she was sinking. Some of the passengers attempted to go on the bridge to get to the boat deck and help lower the boats, as it seemed nothing was being done, but we were ordered back by the Second Steward, who, apparently alone among the ship's officers, kept his head throughout.

No. 1 boat was now being lowered on the port side; it was full of Japanese and Asiatics. When it was flush with the deck the falls broke, the boat capsized, and with all its occupants it was thrown into the sea. One or two, we afterwards heard, were drowned. The passengers now went over to the starboard side, as apparently no more boats were being lowered from the port side, and we did not know whether the raider would start firing again. The No. 1 starboard boat was being lowered; still there was no one to give orders. The passengers themselves saw to it that the women got into this boat first, and helped them in, only the Second Steward standing by to help. The women had to climb the rail and gangway which was lashed thereto, and the boat was so full of gear and tackle that at first it was quite impossible for any one to find a seat in the boat. It was a difficult task for any woman to get into this boat, and everybody was in a great hurry, expecting the firing to recommence, or the ship to sink beneath us, or both; my wife fell in, and in so doing dropped her jewel-case out of her handbag into the bottom of the boat, and it was seen no more that day. The husbands followed their wives into the boat, and several other men among the first-class passengers also clambered in.

Directly after the order to lower away was given, and before any one could settle in the boat, the stern falls broke, and for a second the boat hung from the bow falls vertically, the occupants hanging on to anything they could—a dreadful moment, especially in view of what we had seen happen to the No. 1 port boat a few moments before. Then, immediately afterwards, the bow falls broke, or were cut, the boat dropped into the water with a loud thud and a great splash, and righted itself. We were still alongside the ship when another boat was being swung out and lowered immediately on to our heads. We managed to push off just in time before the other boat, the falls of which also broke, reached the water.

Thus, there was no preparation made for accidents—we might have been living in the times of profoundest peace for all the trouble that had been taken to see that everything was ready in case of accident. Instead of which, nothing was ready—not a very creditable state of affairs for a great steamship company in times such as these, when, thanks to the Huns' ideas of sea chivalry, *any* ship may have to be abandoned at a moment's notice. Some passengers had asked for boat drill when the ship left Singapore, but were told there was no need for it, or for any similar preparations till after Cape Town, which, alas, never was reached. Accordingly passengers had no places given to them in the boats; the boats were not ready, and confusion, instead of order, prevailed. It was nothing short of a miracle that more people were not drowned.

If the ship had only stopped when ordered by signals to do

so, there would have been no firing at all. Even if she had stopped after the warning shots had been fired, no more firing would have taken place and nobody need have left the ship at all. What a vast amount of trouble, fear, anxiety, and damage to life and property might have been saved if only the raider's orders had been obeyed! It seemed too, at the time, that if only the *Hitachi* had turned tail and bolted directly the raider's smoke was seen on the horizon by the officer on watch on the bridge—at the latest this must have been about 1.30—she might have escaped altogether, as she was a much quicker boat than the German. At any rate, she might have tried. Her fate would have been no worse if she had failed to escape, for surely even the Germans could not deny any ship the right to escape if she could effect it. Certainly the seaplane might have taken up the chase, and ordered the *Hitachi* to stop. We heard afterwards that one ship—the *Wairuna*, from New Zealand to San Francisco—had been caught in this way. The seaplane had hovered over her, dropped messages on her deck ordering her to follow the plane to a concealed harbour near, failing which bombs would be dropped to explode the ship. Needless to say, the ship followed these instructions.

"There was no panic, and the women were splendid." How often one has read that in these days of atrocity at sea! We were to realize it now; the women were indeed splendid. There was no crying or screaming or hysteria, or wild inquiries. They were perfectly calm and collected: none of them showed the least fear, even under fire. The women took the matter as coolly as if being shelled and leaving a ship in lifeboats were nothing much out of the ordinary. Their sang-froid was marvellous.

As we thought the ship was slowly sinking, we pushed off from her side as quickly as possible. There were now four lifeboats in the water at some distance from each other. The one in which we were contained about twenty-four persons. There was no officer or member of the crew with us, while another boat contained officers and sailors only. No one in our boat knew where we were to go or what we were to do. One passenger wildly suggested that we should hoist a sail and set sail for Colombo, two days' *steaming* away! Search was made for provisions and water in our boat, but she was so full of people and impedimenta that nothing could be found. It *was* found, however, that water was rapidly coming into the boat, and before long it reached to our knees. The hole which should have been plugged could not be discovered, so for more than an hour some of the men took turns at pulling, and baling the water out with their sun-helmets. This was very hot work, as it must be remembered we were not far from the Equator. Ultimately, however, the hole was found and more or less satisfactorily plugged. Water, however, continued to come in, so baling had still to be proceeded with. An Irish Tommy, going home from Singapore to join up, was in our boat. He was most cheerful and in every way helpful, working hard and pulling all the time. It was he who plugged the hole, and as he was almost the only one among us who seemed to have any useful knowledge about the management of lifeboats, we were very glad to reckon him among our company.

The four boats were now drifting aimlessly about over the sea, when an order was shouted to us, apparently from a Japanese officer in one of the other boats, to tie up with the other three boats. After some time this was accomplished, and the four boats in line drifted on the water. The two steamers had stopped; we did not know what was happening on board either of them, but saw the raider's motor launch going between the raider and her prize, picking up some of the men who had fallen into the sea when the boat capsized. Luckily, the sharks with which these waters are infested had been scared off by the gunfire. We realized, when we were in the lifeboats, what a heavy swell there was on the sea, as both steamers were occasionally hidden from us when we were in the trough of the waves. We were, however, not inconvenienced in any way by the swell, and the lifeboats shipped no water. There was no one in command of any of the boats, and we simply waited to see what was going to happen.

What a sudden, what a dramatic change in our fortunes! One that easily might have been, might even yet be, tragic. At half-past one, less than two hours before, we were comfortably on board a fine ship, absolutely unsuspicious of the least danger. If any of us had thought of the matter at all, we probably imagined we were in the safest part of the ocean. But, at three o'clock, here we were, having undergone the trying ordeal of shell-fire in the interval, drifting helplessly in lifeboats in mid-ocean, all our personal belongings left behind in what we imagined to be a sinking ship, not knowing what fate was in store for us, but naturally, remembering what we had heard of German sea outrages, dreading the very worst.

„Hitachi" passengers and crew in lifeboats after their ship had been shelled. From an enlargement of photo taken on the Wolf by a German officer.

Chapter II. Prisoners on the „Wolf"

Escape in any way was obviously out of the question. At last the raider got under way and began to bear down on us. Things began to look more ugly than ever, and most of us thought that the end had come, and that we were up against an apostle of the "sink the ships and leave no trace" theory—which we had read about in Colombo only a couple of days before—the latest development of "frightfulness." Our minds were not made easier by the seaplane circling above us, ready, as we thought, to administer the final blow to any who might survive being fired on by the raider's guns. It was a most anxious moment for us all, and opinions were very divided as to what was going to happen. One of the ladies remarked that she had no fear, and reminded us that we were all in God's hands, which cheered up some of the drooping hearts and anxious minds. Certainly most of us thought we were soon to look our last upon the world; what other thoughts were in our minds, as we imagined our last moments were so near, will remain unrecorded.

However, to our intense relief, nothing of what we had feared happened, and as the raider came slowly nearer to us—up till now we had not even seen one of the enemy—an officer on the bridge megaphoned us to come alongside. This we did; three boats went astern, and the one in which we were remained near the raider's bows. An officer appeared at the bulwarks and told us to come aboard; women first, then their husbands, then the single men. There was no choice but to obey, but we all felt uneasy in our minds as to what kind of treatment our women were to receive at the hands of the Germans on board.

The ship was rolling considerably, and it is never a pleasant or easy task for a landsman, much less a landswoman, to clamber by a rope-ladder some twenty feet up the side of a rolling ship. However, all the ladies acquitted themselves nobly, some even going up without a rope round their waists. The little Japanese stewardess, terrified, but showing a brave front to the enemy, was the last woman to go up before the men's ascent began. Two German sailors stood at the bulwarks to help us off the rope-ladder into the well deck forward, and by 5.20 we were all aboard, after having spent a very anxious two hours, possibly the most anxious in the lives of most of us. We were all wet, dirty, and dishevelled, and looked sorry objects. One of the passengers, a tall, stout man, was somewhat handicapped by his nether garments slipping down and finally getting in a ruck round his ankles when he was climbing up the ladder on to the raider. A German sailor, to ease his passage, went down the ladder and relieved him of them altogether. He landed on the raider's deck minus this important part of his wardrobe, amid shrieks of laughter from captives and captors.

It was at once evident, directly we got on board, that we were in for kindly treatment. The ship's doctor at once came forward, saluted, and asked who was wounded and required his attention. Most of the passengers—there were only twenty first and about a dozen second class—were in our boat, and among the second-class passengers with us were a few Portuguese soldiers going from Macao to Delagoa Bay.

Some of us were slightly bruised, and all were shaken, but luckily none required medical treatment. Chairs were quickly found for the ladies, the men seated themselves on the hatch, and the German sailors busied themselves bringing tea and cigarettes to their latest captives. We were then left to ourselves for a short time on deck, and just before dark a spruce young Lieutenant came up to me, saluted, and asked me to tell all the passengers that we were to follow him and go aft. We followed him along the ship, which seemed to be very crowded, to the well deck aft, where we met the remaining few passengers and some of the crew of the *Hitachi*. We had evidently come across a new type of Hun. The young Lieutenant was most polite, and courteous and attentive. He apologized profusely for the discomfort which the ladies and ourselves would have to put up with—"But it is war, you know, and your Government is to blame for allowing you to travel when they know a raider is out"—assured us he would do what he could to make us as comfortable as possible, and that we should not be detained more than two or three days. This was the first of a countless number of lies told us by the Germans as to their intentions concerning us.

We had had nothing to eat since tiffin, so we were ordered below to the 'tween decks to have supper. We clambered down a ladder to partake of our first meal as prisoners. What a contrast to the last meal we enjoyed on the *Hitachi*, taken in comfort and apparent security! (But, had we known it, we were doomed even then, for the raider's seaplane had been up and seen us at 11 a.m., had reported our position to the raider, and announced 3 p.m. as the time for our capture. Our captors were not far out! It was between 2.30 and 3 when we were taken.) The meal consisted of black bread and raw ham, with hot tea in a tin can, into which we dipped our cups. We sat around on wooden benches, in a small partitioned-off space, and noticed that the crockery on which the food was served had been taken from other ships captured—one of the Burns Philp Line, and one of the Union Steamship Company of New Zealand. Some of the Japanese officers and crew were also in the 'tween decks—later on the Japanese Captain appeared (we had not seen him since he left the *Hitachi* saloon after tiffin), and he was naturally very down and distressed—and some of the German sailors came and spoke to us. Shortly after, the young Lieutenant came down and explained why the raider, which the German sailors told us was the *Wolf*, had fired on us. We then learnt for the first time that many persons had been killed outright by the firing—another direct result of the *Hitachi's* failure to obey the raider's orders to stop. It was impossible to discover how many. There must have been about a dozen, as the total deaths numbered sixteen, all Japanese or Indians; the latest death from wounds occurred on October 28th, while one or two died while we were on the *Wolf*. The Lieutenant, who we afterwards learnt was in charge of the prisoners, told us that the *Wolf* had signalled us to stop, and not to use our wireless or our gun, for the *Hitachi* mounted a gun on her poop for the submarine zone. He asserted that the *Hitachi* hoisted a signal that she understood the order, but that she tried to use her wireless, that she brought herself into position to fire on the *Wolf*, and that preparations were being made to use her gun. If the *Hitachi* had manœuvred at all, it was simply so that she should not present her broadside as a target for a torpedo from the raider.

The Germans professed deep regret at the *Hitachi's* action and at the loss of life caused, the first occasion, they said—and, we believe, with truth—on which lives had been lost since the *Wolf's* cruise began. The *Wolf*, however, they said, had no choice but to fire and put the *Hitachi* gun out of action. This she failed to do, as the shooting was distinctly poor, with the exception of the shot aimed at the wireless room, which went straight through the room, without exploding there or touching the operator, and exploded near the funnel, killing most of the crew who met their deaths while running to help lower the boats. The other shots had all struck the ship in the second-class quarters astern. One had gone right through the cabin of the Second Steward, passing just over his bunk—where he had been asleep a minute before—and through the side of the ship. Others had done great damage to the ship's structure aft, but none had gone anywhere near the gun or ammunition house on the poop. I saw afterwards some photos the Germans had taken of the gun as they said they found it when they went on board. These photos showed the gun with the breech open, thus proving, so the Germans said, that the Japanese had been preparing to use the gun. In reality, of course, it proved nothing of the sort; it is more than likely that the Germans opened the breech themselves before they took this photograph, as they had to produce some evidence to justify their firing on the *Hitachi*. But whether the Japanese opened the gun breech and prepared to use the gun or not, it is quite certain that the *Hitachi* never fired a shot at the *Wolf*, though the Germans have since asserted that she did so. It was indeed very lucky for us that she did not fire—had she done so and even missed the *Wolf*, it is quite certain the *Wolf* would have torpedoed the *Hitachi* and sent us to the bottom.

It was very hot in the 'tween decks, although a ventilating fan was at work there, and after our meal we were all allowed to go on deck for some fresh air. About eight o'clock, however, the single men of military age were again sent below for the night, while the married couples and a few sick and elderly men were allowed to remain on deck, which armed guards patrolled all night. It was a cool moonlight night. We had nothing but what we stood up in, so we lay down in chairs as we were, and that night slept—or rather did not sleep—under one of the *Wolf's* guns. Throughout the night we were steaming gently, and from time to time we saw the *Hitachi* still afloat, and steaming along at a considerable distance from us. During the night, one of the passengers gifted with a highly cultivated imagination—who had previously related harrowing details of his escape from a shell which he said had smashed his and my cabin immediately after we left them, but which were afterwards found to be quite intact—told me he had seen the *Hitachi* go down at 2.30 in the morning. So she evidently must have come up again, for she was still in sight just before daybreak! Soon after daybreak next morning, the men were allowed to go aft under the poop for a wash, with a very limited supply of water, and the ladies had a portion of the 'tween decks to themselves for a short time. Breakfast, consisting of black bread, canned meat, and tea, was then brought to us on deck by the German sailors, and we were left to ourselves on the well deck for some time. The Commander sent down a message conveying his compliments to the ladies, saying he hoped they had had a good night and were none the worse for their experiences. He assured us all that we should be in no danger on his ship and that he would do what he could to make us as comfortable as possible under the circumstances. But, we were reminded again, this is war. Indeed it was, and we had good reason to know it now, even if the war had not touched us closely before.

How vividly every detail of this scene stands out in our memories! The brilliant tropical sunshine, the calm blue sea, the ship crowded in every part, the activity everywhere evident, and—we were prisoners! The old familiar petition of the Litany, "to shew Thy pity upon all prisoners and captives," had suddenly acquired for us a fuller meaning and a new significance. What would the friends we had left behind, our people at home, be thinking—if they only knew! But they were in blissful ignorance of our fate—communication of any kind with the world outside the little one of the *Wolf* was quite impossible.

There seemed to be literally hundreds of prisoners on and under the poop, and the whole ship, as far as we could see, presented a scene of the greatest activity. Smiths were at work on the well deck, with deafening din hammering and cutting steel plates with which to repair the *Hitachi*; mechanics were working at the seaplane, called the *Wölfchen*, which was kept on the well deck between her flights; prisoners were exercising on the poop, and the armed guards were patrolling constantly among them and near us on the well deck. The guards wore revolvers and side-arms, but did not appear at all particular in the matter of uniform. Names of various ships appeared on their caps, while some had on their caps only the words "Kaiserliche Marine." Some were barefoot, some wore singlets and shorts, while some even dispensed with the former. Most of the crew at work wore only shorts, and, as one of the lady prisoners remarked, the ship presented a rather unusual exhibition of the European male torso! There seemed to have been a lavish distribution of the Iron Cross among the ship's company. Every officer we saw and many of the crew as well wore the ribbon of the coveted decoration.

Some German officers came aft to interrogate us; they were all courteous and sympathetic, and I took the opportunity of mentioning to the young Lieutenant the loss of my wife's jewels in the lifeboat, and he assured me he would have the boat searched, and if the jewels were found they should be restored.

The Japanese dhobi had died from wounds during the night, and he was buried in the morning; nearly all the German officers, from the Commander downwards, attending in full uniform. The Japanese Captain and officers also attended, and some kind of funeral service in Japanese was held.

Officers and men were very busy on the upper deck—we were much impressed by the great number of men on board—and we noticed a lady prisoner, a little girl—evidently a great pet with the German sailors and officers—some civilian prisoners, and some military prisoners in khaki on the upper deck, but we were not allowed to communicate with them. There were also a few Tommies in khaki among the prisoners aft. It was very hot on the well deck, and for some hours we had no shelter from the blazing sun. Later on, a small awning was rigged up and we got a little protection, and one or two parasols were forthcoming for the use of the ladies. A small wild pig, presumably taken from some Pacific island when the *Wolf* had sent a boat ashore, was wandering around the well deck, a few dachshunds were wriggling along the upper deck, and a dozen or so pigeons had their home on the boat deck. During the morning the sailors were allowed to bring us cooling drinks from time to time in one or two glass jugs (which the Asiatics and Portuguese always made a grab at first), and both officers and men did all they could to render our position as bearable as possible. The men amongst us were also allowed to go to the ship's canteen and buy smokes. We were steaming gently in a westerly direction all day, occasionally passing quite close to some small islands and banks of sand, a quite picturesque scene. The sea was beautifully calm and blue, and on the shores of these banks, to which we sailed quite close, the water took on colours of exquisite hues of the palest and tenderest blue and green, as it rippled gently over coral and golden sands.

Tiffin, consisting of rice, and bacon and beans, was dealt out to us on deck at midday, and the afternoon passed in the same way as the morning. The *Wolf*'s chief officer, a hearty, elderly man, came aft to speak to us. He chaffed us about our oarsmanship in the lifeboats, saying the appearance of our oars wildly waving reminded him of the sails of a windmill. "Never use your wireless or your gun," he said, "and you'll come to no harm from a German raider."

The long hot day seemed endless, but by about five o'clock the two ships arrived in an atoll, consisting of about fifteen small islands, and the *Hitachi* there dropped anchor. The *Wolf* moved up alongside, and the two ships were lashed together. Supper, consisting of tinned fruit and rice, was served out at 5.30, and we were then told that the married couples and one or two elderly men were to return to the *Hitachi* that night. So with some difficulty we clambered from the upper deck of the *Wolf* to the boat deck of the *Hitachi* and returned to find our cabins just as we had left them in a great hurry the day before. We had not expected to go on board the *Hitachi* again, and never thought we should renew acquaintance with our personal belongings. We ourselves were particularly sad about this, as we had brought away from Siam, after twenty years' residence there, many things which would be quite irreplaceable. We were therefore very glad to know they were not all lost to us. But we congratulated ourselves that the greater part of our treasures gathered there had been left behind safely stored in the Bank and in a go-down in Bangkok.

Chapter III. Back to the „Hitachi Maru"

The *Hitachi* was now a German ship, the Prize Captain was in command, and German sailors replaced the Japanese, who had all been transferred to the *Wolf*. The German Captain spoke excellent English, and expressed a wish to do all he could to make us as comfortable on board as we had been before. He also told us to report at once to him if anything were missing from our cabins. (He informed us later that he had lived some years in Richmond — he evidently knew the neighbourhood quite well — and that he had been a member of the Richmond Tennis Club!) There was of course considerable confusion on board; the deck was in a state of dirt and chaos, littered with books and chairs, and some parts of it were an inch or two deep in water, and we found next morning that the bathrooms and lavatories were not in working order, as the pipes supplying these places had been shot away when the ship was shelled. This state of affairs prevailed for the next few days, and the men passengers themselves had to do what was necessary in these quarters and haul sea-water aboard. The next morning the transference of coal, cargo, and ship's stores from the *Hitachi* to the *Wolf* began, and went on without cessation day and night for the next five days. One of the German officers came over and took photos of the passengers in groups, and others frequently took snapshots of various incidents and of each other on different parts of the ship.

We know now that we were then anchored *in a British possession*, one of the southernmost groups of the Maldive Islands! Some of the islands were inhabited, and small sailing boats came out to the *Wolf*, presumably with provisions of some kind. We were, of course, not allowed to speak to any of the islanders, who came alongside the *Wolf*, and were not allowed alongside the *Hitachi*. On one occasion even, the doctor of the *Wolf* went in the ship's motor launch to one of the islands to attend the wife of one of the native chiefs! On the next day — the 28th — all the *Hitachi* passengers returned on board her, and at the same time some of the Japanese stewards returned, but they showed no inclination to work as formerly. Indeed, the German officers had no little difficulty in dealing with them. They naturally felt very sore at the deaths of so many of their countrymen at the hands of the Germans, and they did as little work as possible. The stewards were said to be now paid by the Germans, but as they were no longer under the command of their own countrymen, they certainly did not put themselves out to please their new masters.

With their usual thoroughness, the Germans one day examined all our passports and took notes of our names, ages, professions, maiden names of married ladies, addresses, and various other details. My passport described me as "Principal of Training College for Teachers." So I was forthwith dubbed "Professor" by the Germans, and from this time henceforth my wife and I were called Frau Professor and Herr Professor, and this certainly led the sailors to treat us with more respect than they might otherwise have done. One young man, who had on his passport his photo taken in military uniform, was, however, detained on the *Wolf* as a military prisoner. He was asked by a German officer if he were going home to fight. He replied that he certainly was, and pluckily added, "I wish I were fighting now."

On October 1st the married prisoners from the *Wolf*, together with three Australian civilian prisoners over military age, a Colonel of the Australian A.M.C., a Major of the same corps, and his wife, with an Australian stewardess, some young boys, and a few old sea captains and mates, were sent on board the *Hitachi*. They had all been taken off earlier prizes captured and sunk by the *Wolf*. The Australians had been captured on August 6th from the s.s. *Matunga* from Sydney to what was formerly German New Guinea, from which latter place they had been only a few hours distant. An American captain, with his wife and little girl, had been captured on the barque *Beluga*, from San Francisco to Newcastle, N.S.W., on July 9th. All the passengers transferred were given cabins on board the *Hitachi*. We learnt from these passengers that the *Wolf* was primarily a mine-layer, and that she had laid mines at Cape Town, Bombay, Colombo, and off the Australian and New Zealand coasts. She had sown her last crop of mines, 110 in number, off the approaches to Singapore before she proceeded to the Indian Ocean to lie in wait for the *Hitachi*. Altogether she had sown five hundred mines.

During her stay in the Maldives the *Wolf* sent up her seaplane—or, as the Germans said, "the bird"—every morning about six, and she returned about eight. To all appearances the coast was clear, and the *Wolf* consequently anticipated no interference or unwelcome attention from any of our cruisers. Two of them, the *Venus* and the *Doris*, we had seen at anchor in Colombo harbour during our stay there, but it was apparently thought not worth while to send any escort with the *Hitachi*, though the value of her cargo was said to run into millions sterling; and evidently the convoy system had not yet been adopted in Eastern waters. A Japanese cruiser was also in Colombo harbour when we arrived there, preceded by mine-sweepers, on September 24th. The *Hitachi* Captain and senior officers visited her before she sailed away on the 25th. The Germans on the *Wolf* told us that they heard her wireless call when later on she struck one of their mines off Singapore, but the Japanese authorities have since denied that one of their cruisers struck a mine there.

The *Wolf* remained alongside us till the morning of October 3rd, when she sailed away at daybreak, leaving us anchored in the centre of the atoll. It was a great relief to us when she departed; she kept all the breeze off our side of the ship, so that the heat in our cabin was stifling, and it was in addition very dark; the noise of coaling and shifting cargo was incessant, and the roaring of the water between the two ships most disturbing. Before she sailed away the Prize Captain handed to my wife most of her jewels which had been recovered from the bottom of our lifeboat. As many of these were Siamese jewellery and unobtainable now, we were very rejoiced to obtain possession of them again, but many rings were missing and were never recovered.

The falls of the lifeboats were all renewed, and on October 5th we had places assigned to us in the lifeboats, and rules and regulations were drawn up for the "detained enemy subjects" on board the *Hitachi*. They were as follows:—

RULES AND REGULATIONS FOR ON BOARD THE GERMAN AUXILIARY SHIP "HITACHI MARU" DETAINED ENEMY SUBJECTS (d.e.s.).

1. Everybody on board is under martial law, and any offence is liable to be punished by same.

2. All orders given by the Commander, First Officer, or any of the German crew on duty are to be strictly obeyed.

3. After the order "Schiff abblenden" every evening at sunset no lights may be shown on deck or through portholes, etc., that are visible from outside.

4. The order "Alle Mann in die Boote" will be made known by continuous ringing of the ship's bell and sounding of gongs. Everybody hurries to his boat with the lifebelt and leaves the ship. Everybody is allowed to take one small bag previously packed.

5. Nobody is allowed to go on the boat deck beyond the smoke-room. All persons living in first-class cabins are to stay amidships, and are not allowed to go aft without special permission; all persons living aft are to stay aft.

6. The Japanese crew is kept only for the comfort of the one-time passengers, and is to be treated considerately, as they are also d.e.s.

7. The d.e.s. are not allowed to talk with the crew.

At sea, October 6, 1917.
Kommando S.M.H. *Hitachi Maru,*
C. Rose,
Lt. z. See & Kommandant.

Lieutenant Rose very kindly told me that as I was leaving the East for good and therefore somewhat differently situated from the other passengers, he would allow me to take in the lifeboat, in addition to a handbag, a cabin trunk packed with the articles from Siam I most wanted to save.

It was evident from this that the Germans intended sinking the ship if we came across a British or Allied war vessel. We were of course unarmed, as the Germans had removed the *Hitachi* gun to the *Wolf,* but the German Captain anticipated no difficulty on this score, and assured me that it was the intention of the Commander of the *Wolf* that we should be landed in a short time with all our baggage at a neutral port with a stone pier. We took this to mean a port in either Sumatra or Java, and we were buoyed up with this hope for quite a considerable time. But, alas, like many more of the assurances given to us, it was quite untrue.

There were now on board 131 souls, of whom twenty-nine were passengers. On Saturday, October 6th, the seaplane returned in the afternoon and remained about half an hour, when she again flew away. She brought a message of evidently great importance, for whereas it had been the intention of our Captain to sail away on the following afternoon, he weighed anchor the next morning and left the atoll. He had considerable trouble with the anchor before starting, and did not get away till nearly eight o'clock, instead of at daybreak. Evidently something was coming to visit the atoll; though it was certain nothing could be looking for us, as our capture could not then have been known, and there could have been no communication between the Maldives and Ceylon, or the mainland. Before and for some days after we sailed, the ship was cleaned and put in order, the cargo properly stowed, and the bunkers trimmed by the German crew, aided by some neutrals who had been taken prisoner from other ships. Some of the sailors among the prize crew were good enough to give us some pieces of the *Wolf*'s shrapnel found on the *Hitachi*, relics which were eagerly sought after by the passengers.

The passengers were now under armed guards, but were at perfect liberty to do as they pleased, and the relations between them and the German officers and crew were quite friendly. Deck games were indulged in as before our capture, and the German Captain took part in them. Time, nevertheless, hung very heavily on our hands, but many a pleasant hour was spent in the saloon with music and singing. One of the Australian prisoners was a very good singer and pianist, and provided very enjoyable entertainment for us. The Captain, knowing that I had some songs with me, one afternoon asked me to sing. I was not feeling like singing, so I declined. "Shot at dawn!" he said. "Ready now," I replied. "No!" said he. "I can't oblige you now. Either at dawn, for disobedience to Captain's orders, or not at all." So it was made the latter! On Sunday evenings, after the six o'clock "supper," a small party met in the saloon to sing a few favourite hymns, each one choosing the ones he or she liked best. This little gathering was looked forward to by those who took part in it, as it formed a welcome break in the ordinary monotonous life on board.

The only Japanese left on board were some stewards, cooks, and the stewardess. A German chief mate and chief engineer replaced the Japanese, and other posts previously held by the Japanese were filled by Germans and neutrals. The times of meals were changed, and we no longer enjoyed the good meals we had had before our capture, as most of the good food had been transferred to the *Wolf*. *Chota-hazri* was done away with, except for the ladies; the meals became much simpler, menus were no longer necessary, and the Japanese cooks took no more trouble with the preparation of the food.

However, on the whole we were not so badly off, though on a few occasions there was really not enough to eat, and some of the meat was tainted, as the freezing apparatus had got out of order soon after the ship was captured.

There was no longer any laundry on board, as the dhobi had been killed. Amateur efforts by some Japanese stewards were not successful, so the passengers had to do their own washing as best they could. They were helped in this by some of the young boys sent on board. The walls of the alley-ways were plastered with handkerchiefs, etc., drying in Chinese fashion, the alley-ways became drying-rooms for other garments hung on the rails, and ironing with electric irons was done on the saloon tables. Some of the men passengers soon became expert ironers.

We steamed gently on a south-westerly course for about five days, and on the succeeding day, October 12th, changed our course many times, going north-east at 6.30 a.m., south-east at 12.30 p.m., north-east again at 4 p.m., and north at 6.30 p.m., evidently waiting for something and killing time, as we were going dead slow all day. The next morning we had stopped entirely; we sighted smoke at 10.20 a.m. — it was, of course, the *Wolf*, met by appointment at that particular time and place. She came abreast of us about 11.20 a.m., and we sailed on parallel courses for the rest of the day. She was unaccompanied by a new prize, and we were glad to think she had been unsuccessful in her hunt for further prey. She remained in company with us all next day, Sunday, and about 5 p.m. moved closer up, and after an exchange of signals we both changed courses and the *Wolf* sheered off, and to our great relief we saw her no more for several days. There was always the hope that when away from us she would be seen and captured by an Allied cruiser, and always the fear that, failing such happy consummation, when she came back to us we might again be put on board her. The Germans seemed to have a perfect mania for taking photographs—we were, of course, not allowed to take any, and cameras were even taken away from us—and one day Lieutenant Rose showed me photos of various incidents of the *Wolf's* cruise, including those of the sinkings of various ships. I asked him how he, a sailor, felt when he saw good ships being sent to the bottom. Did he feel no remorse, no regret? He admitted he did, but the Germans, he said, had no choice in the matter. They had no port to which they could take their prizes — this, of course, was the fault of the British! (I saw, too, on this day a photo of the *Hitachi* flying the German flag, and one showing the damage sustained by her from the *Wolf's* firing. There were ugly holes in the stern quarters, but all above the water-line.) The German officers would take with them to Germany hundreds of pictures giving a complete photographic record of the *Wolf's* expedition.

We cruised about again after the *Wolf* had left us for a couple of days, and on the 17th were stationary all day. Several sharks were seen around the ship, and the German sailors caught two or three fairly large ones during the day and got them on board. One particularly ravenous shark made off with the bait three times, and was dragged halfway up the ship's side on each occasion. So greedy was he that he returned to the charge for the fourth time, seized the bait, and was this time successfully hauled on board. On the 18th the sea was rough, and we were gently steaming to keep the ship's head to the seas, and on the following day we again changed our course many times. Saturday morning, October 20th, again saw the *Wolf* in sight at 6.30. She was still alone, and we proceeded on parallel courses, passing about midday a few white reefs with breakers sweeping over them. Shortly after, we came in sight of many other reefs, most of which were quite bare, but there were a few trees and a little vegetation on the largest of them, and at 2 p.m. we anchored, and the *Wolf* tied up alongside us at a snug and sheltered spot. We were almost surrounded by large and small coral reefs, against which we could see and hear the breakers dashing. It was a beautiful anchorage, and the waters were evidently well known to the Germans. Some of the seafaring men amongst us told us we were in the Cargados Carajos Reef, south-east of the Seychelles, and that we were anchored near the Nazareth Bank.

Chapter IV. The Germans Sink Their Prize

So confident did the Germans feel of their security that they stayed in this neighbourhood from October 20th to November 7th, only once—on October 28th—moving a few hundred yards away from their original anchorage, and although a most vigilant lookout was kept from the crow's nest on the *Wolf*, the seaplane was not sent up once to scout during the whole of that time. Coal, cargo, and stores were transferred from the *Hitachi* to the *Wolf*, and the work went on day and night with just as much prospect of interference as there would have been if the *Wolf* had been loading cargo from a wharf in Hamburg in peace-time. The coolness and impudence of the whole thing amazed us.

But one day, October 22nd, was observed as a holiday. It was Lieutenant Rose's birthday, and, incidentally, the Kaiserin's also. So no loading or coaling was done, but the band on the *Wolf*—most of the members with the minimum of clothing and nearly all with faces and bodies black with coal-dust—lined up and gave a musical performance of German patriotic airs.

Every day we looked, but in vain, for signs of help in the shape of a friendly cruiser, but the Germans proceeded with their high-seas robbery undisturbed and unalarmed. The *Hitachi* had a valuable cargo of rubber, silk, tea, tin, copper, antimony, hides, cocoa-nut, and general stores, and it was indeed maddening to see all these cases marked for Liverpool and London being transferred to the capacious maw of the *Wolf* for the use of our enemies. The silk came in very handy—the Germans used a great deal of it to make new wings for their "bird." The seaplane did not, of course, take off from the *Wolf*'s deck, which was far too crowded. She was lowered over the side by means of the winch, and towed a little distance by the motor launch before rising. On her return she was taken in tow again by the launch and then lifted aboard to her quarters. She made some beautiful flights. The Germans told us that when the *Wolf* was mine-laying in Australian waters the seaplane made a flight over Sydney. What a commotion there would have been in the southern hemisphere if she had launched some of her bolts from the blue on the beautiful

Australian city!

On October 28th a Japanese sailor, wounded at the time of the *Hitachi's* capture, died on the *Wolf*. This was the last death from wounds inflicted on that day. His body was brought over to the *Hitachi*—once again all the German officers, from the Commander downwards, including the two doctors, appeared in full uniform to attend the funeral service. The Japanese Captain and officers also came over from the *Wolf*, and the body was committed to the sea from the poop of the *Hitachi*.

We had now been prisoners more than a month, and various rumours came into circulation about this time as to what was to happen to us. The most likely thing was, if the *Wolf* did not secure another prize, that the *Hitachi* would be sunk and all of us transferred to the *Wolf* once more. It was certain, however, that the Germans did not want us on the *Wolf* again, and still more certain that we did not want to go. They regarded us, especially the women, as a nuisance on board their ship, which was already more than comfortably full. In addition, some of the German officers who had before given up their cabins to some of the married couple prisoners naturally did not want to do so again, as it meant that all the officers' quarters became very cramped. The German doctor, too, protested against further crowding of the *Wolf*, but all these protests were overruled.

There was talk of leaving the *Hitachi* where she was, with some weeks' stores on board, with her coal exhausted and her wireless dismantled, the *Wolf* to send out a wireless in a few weeks' time as to our condition and whereabouts. If this had happened, there was further talk among us of a boat expedition to the Seychelles to effect an earlier rescue. The expedition would have been in charge of the American Captain, some of whose crew—neutrals—were helping to work the *Hitachi*. There was also mentioned another scheme of taking the *Hitachi* near Mauritius, sending all her prisoners and German officers and crew off in boats at nightfall to the island, and then blowing up the ship. Lieutenant Rose admitted that if he and his crew were interned in a British possession he knew they would all be well treated. But all these plans came to nothing, and as day by day went by and the *Wolf*, for reasons best known to herself, did not go out after another prize, though the Germans knew and told us what steamers were about—and in more than one case we knew they were correct—it became evident that the *Hitachi* would have to be destroyed, as she had not enough coal to carry on with, and we should all have to be sent on to the *Wolf*.

But the married men protested vigorously against having their wives put in danger of shell-fire from a British or Allied cruiser, and on October 30th sent the following petition to the Commander of the *Wolf*:—

"We, the undersigned detained enemy subjects travelling with our wives, some of whom have already been exposed to shell-fire, and the remainder to the risk thereof, and have suffered many weeks' detention on board, respectfully beg that no women be transferred to the auxiliary cruiser, thereby exposing them to a repetition of the grave dangers they have already run. We earnestly trust that some means may be found by which consideration may be shown to all the women on board by landing them safely without their incurring further peril. We take this opportunity of expressing our gratitude for the treatment we have received since our capture, and our sincere appreciation of the courtesy and consideration shown us by every officer and man from your ship with whom we have been brought in contact."

He sent back a verbal message that there was no alternative but to put us all, women included, on the *Wolf*, as the *Hitachi* had no coal, but that they should be landed at a neutral port from the next boat caught, if she had any coal.

We were still not satisfied with this, and I again protested to our Captain against what was equivalent to putting our women in a German first-line trench to be shot by our own people. He replied that we need have no anxiety on that score. "We know exactly where all your cruisers are, we pick up all their wireless messages, and we shall never see or go anywhere near one of them." Whether the Germans did know this, or hear our ships' wireless I cannot tell, but it is certainly true that we never, between September and February, saw a British or Allied war vessel of any sort or kind, or even the smoke of one (with the single exception to be mentioned later), although during that time we travelled from Ceylon to the Cape, and the whole length of the Atlantic Ocean from below 40° S. to the shores of Iceland, and thence across to the shores of Norway and Denmark. But notwithstanding the Captain's assurance, we still felt it possible that on the *Wolf* we might be fired on by an Allied cruiser, and some of us set about settling up our affairs, and kept such documents always on our persons, so that if we were killed and our bodies found by a friendly vessel our last wishes concerning our affairs might be made known. I wrote my final directions on the blank sheet of my Letter of Credit on the Hong-Kong and Shanghai Bank, which, after being cancelled, I now keep as a relic of a most anxious time when I was a very unwilling guest of the Kaiser's Navy.

The food on the *Hitachi* was now getting poorer and poorer. There was no longer any fruit, cheese, vegetables, coffee, or jam. All the eggs were bad, and when opened protested with a lively squeak; only a very little butter remained, the beer was reserved for the ship's officers, iced water and drinks were no longer obtainable, and the meat became more and more unpleasant. One morning at breakfast, the porridge served had evidently made more than a nodding acquaintance with some kerosene, and was consequently quite uneatable. So most of the passengers sent it away in disgust. But one of them, ever anxious to please his captors, "wolfed" his allowance notwithstanding. He constantly assured the Germans that the food was always ample and excellent, no matter how little or bad it was. When Lieutenant Rose came down to breakfast that morning, we were all waiting to see what he would do with his kerosene porridge. He took one spoonful and, amid roars of laughter from us all, called for the steward to take it away at once. Our hero looked as if he were sorry he had not done the same! On the *Wolf* the food was still poorer, and beri-beri broke out on the raider. A case of typhoid also appeared on the *Wolf*, and the German doctors thereupon inoculated every man, woman, and child on both ships against typhoid. We had heard before of German "inoculations," and some of us had nasty forebodings as to the results. But protests were of no avail—every one had to submit. The first inoculation took place on November 1st and the next on November 11th, and some of the people were inoculated a third time. The Senior Doctor of the *Wolf*, on hearing that I had come from Siam, told me that a Siamese Prince had once attended his classes at a German University. He remembered his name, and, strangely enough, this Prince was the Head of the University of Siam with which I had so recently been connected!

One night, while the ships were lashed alongside, a great uproar arose on both ships. The alarm was given, orders were shouted, revolvers and side-arms were hastily assumed, and sailors commenced rushing and shouting from all parts of both ships. Most of us were scared, not knowing what had happened. It appeared that a German sailor had fallen down between the two ships; his cries, of course, added to the tumult, but luckily he was dragged up without being much injured. We could not help wondering, if such a commotion were made at such a small accident, what would happen if a cruiser came along and the real alarm were given. The ship would bid fair to become a veritable madhouse—evidently the nerves of all the Germans were very much on edge. The only thing for the prisoners to do was to get out of the way as much as possible, and retire to their cabins.

In addition to the transference of coal and cargo which went on without cessation, day and night, our ship was gradually being stripped. Bunks and cabin fittings, heating apparatus, pianos, bookcases, brass and rubber stair-treads, bed and table linen, ceiling and table electric fans, clocks, and all movable fittings were transferred to the *Wolf*, and our ship presented a scene of greater destruction every day. The Germans were excellent shipbreakers. Much of the cargo could not be taken on board the *Wolf*; it was not wanted, and there was no room for it, and some of this, especially some fancy Japanese goods, clothes, gloves, and toys, was broached by the sailors, and some was left untouched in the holds. The Prize Captain secured for himself as a trophy a large picture placed at the head of the saloon stairs of the *Hitachi*. This represented a beautiful Japanese woodland scene, embossed and painted on velvet. The Germans said the *Hitachi* was due to arrive at her destination between November 4th and November 8th. They told us she would still do so, but that the destination would be slightly different—not Liverpool, but Davy Jones's locker! Some of the prisoners aft had seen several ships sunk by the *Wolf*. They told us that on more than one such occasion a German officer had gone down among them whistling "Britannia Rules the Waves." They will perhaps admit by this time that she does so still, the *Wolf* notwithstanding!

Longing eyes had been cast on the notice published by the Germans concerning rules and regulations on board, and most of us determined to get possession of it. When first fixed on the notice-board it had been blown down, and recovered by a German sailor. It was then framed and again exhibited. Later on, it was again taken out of its frame and pinned up. It remained on the notice-board till the day before the *Hitachi* was sunk. After supper that evening I was lucky enough to find it still there, so removed it, and have kept it as a memento of the time when I was a "detained enemy subject."

The boats were all lashed down, the hatches the same, and every precaution taken to prevent wreckage floating away when the vessel was sunk. On the afternoon of November 5th the Germans shifted all the passengers' heavy luggage on to the *Wolf*, and we were told we should have to leave the *Hitachi* and go on board the *Wolf* at 1 p.m. the next day. We were told that our baggage would all be opened and passed through a fumigating chamber, and that we ourselves would have to be thoroughly fumigated before being "allowed" to mix with the company on the *Wolf*. But this part of the programme was omitted.

The *Hitachi* was now in a sad condition; her glory was indeed departed and her end very near. We had our last meal in her stripped saloon that day at noon, and at one o'clock moved over on to the *Wolf*, the German sailors, aided by some neutrals, carrying our light cabin luggage for us. The Commander of the *Wolf* himself superintended our crossing from one ship to the other, and he had had a gangway specially made for us. We felt more like prisoners than ever! The crew and their belongings, the Japanese stewards and theirs, moved over to the *Wolf* in the afternoon, and at 5 p.m. on November 6th the *Wolf* sheered off, leaving the *Hitachi* deserted, but for the German Captain and officers, and the bombing party who were to send her to the bottom next day.

Both ships remained where they were for the night, abreast of and about four hundred yards distant from each other. At 9 a.m. on November 7th they moved off and manœuvred. The Germans did not intend to sink the *Hitachi* where she was, but in deep water. To do this they had to sail some distance from the Nazareth Bank. The *Hitachi* hoisted the German Imperial Navy flag, and performed a kind of naval goose-step for the delectation of the *Wolf*. At 1 p.m. the flag was hauled down, both ships stopped, and the *Hitachi* blew off steam for the last time.

There were still a few people on her, and the *Wolf*'s motor launch made three trips between the two ships before the German Captain and bombing officer left the *Hitachi*. Three bombs had been placed for her destruction, one forward outside the ship on the starboard side, one amidships inside, and one aft on the port side outside the ship. At 1.33 p.m. the Captain arrived alongside the *Wolf*, at 1.34 the first bomb exploded with a dull subdued roar, sending up a high column of water; the explosion of the other bombs followed at intervals of a minute, so that by 1.36 the last bomb had exploded. All on the *Wolf* now stood watching the *Hitachi*'s last struggle with the waves, a struggle which, thanks to her murderers, could have but one end; and the German officers stood on the *Wolf*'s deck taking photos at different stages of the tragedy. There the two ships now rested, the murderer and the victim, alone on the ocean, with no help for the one and no avenging justice for the other. The *Wolf* was secure from all interference—nothing could avert the final tragedy. The many witnesses who would have helped the victim were powerless; we could but stand and watch with impotent fury and great sorrow and pity the inevitable fate to which the *Hitachi* was doomed, and of which the captors and captives on the *Wolf* were the only witnesses. But one man among us refused to look on—the Japanese Captain refused to be a spectator of the wilful destruction of his ship, which had so long been his home. Her sinking meant for him the utter destruction of his hopes and an absolute end to his career. The struggle was a long one—it was pathetic beyond words to watch it, and there was a choky feeling in many a throat on the *Wolf*—for some time it even seemed as if the *Hitachi* were going to snatch one more victory from the sea; she seemed to be defying the efforts of the waves to devour her, as, gently rolling, she shook herself free from the gradually encroaching water; but she was slowly getting lower in the water, and just before two o'clock there were signs that she was settling fast. Her well deck forward was awash; we could see the waves breaking on it; exactly at two o'clock her bows went under, and soon her funnel was surrounded with swirling water; it disappeared, and with her propellers high in the air she dived slowly and slantingly down to her great grave, and at one minute past two the sea closed over her. Twenty-five minutes had elapsed since the explosion of the last bomb. The Germans said she and her cargo were worth a million sterling when she went down.

Nippon Yusen Kaisha S.S. „Hitachi Maru".

There was great turmoil on the sea for some time after the ship disappeared; the ammunition house on the poop floated away, a fair amount of wreckage also came away, an oar shot up high into the air from one of the hatches, the sodium lights attached to one of the lifebuoys ignited and ran along the water, and then the *Wolf*, exactly like a murderer making sure that the struggles of his victim had finally ceased, moved away from the scene of her latest crime. Never shall we forget the tragedy of that last half-hour in the life of the *Hitachi Maru*.

Thus came to an end the second of the Nippon Yushen Kaisha fleet bearing the name of *Hitachi Maru*. The original ship of that name had been sunk by the Russians in the Russo-Japanese War. Our ill-fated vessel had taken her place. It will savour of tempting Providence if another ship ever bears her unfortunate name, and no sailor could be blamed for refusing to sail in her.

Chapter V. Life on the „Wolf"

Life on the *Wolf* was very different from life on the *Hitachi*. To begin with, all the single men of military age from the *Hitachi* were accommodated on the 'tween decks, and slept in hammocks which they had to sling themselves. The elder men among them slept in bunks taken from the *Hitachi*, but the quarters of all in the 'tween decks were very restricted; there was no privacy, no convenience, and only a screen divided the European and Japanese quarters. The condition of our fellow-countrymen from the *Hitachi* was now the reverse of enviable, though it was a great deal better than that of the crews of the captured ships, who were "accommodated" under the poop—where the Captains and officers captured had quarters to themselves—and exercised on the poop and well deck, the port side of which was reserved for the Japanese. The Germans did not forbid us to enter the quarters where our fellow-passengers were confined, but it was obvious that they did not like our doing so, after the lies they had told us concerning the wonderful alterations made in these quarters for their prisoners' "comfort." One day I managed to sneak unobserved into the prisoners' quarters under the poop in the 'tween decks, where hundreds of men were confined, but I had the misfortune to run up against the Lieutenant in charge and was promptly ordered out before I could have a good look round. But I had seen enough! Both the men under the poop and our fellow-passengers had armed guards over them—those guarding the latter were good fellows and quite friendly and helpful to their charges.

There were now more than four hundred prisoners on board, mostly British, some of whom had been captured in the February previous, as the *Wolf* had left Germany in November 1916, the *Hitachi* being the tenth prize taken. The condition in which these prisoners lived cannot be too strongly condemned. The heat in the tropics was insufferable, the overcrowding abominable, and on the poop there was hardly room to move. While anchored near Sunday Island in the Pacific some months earlier, two of the British prisoners taken from the first prize captured managed to escape. Their absence was not noticed by the

Germans till a fortnight later, as up to then there had been no daily roll-call, an omission which was at once rectified directly these two men were noted missing. As a punishment, the prisoners aft were no longer allowed to exercise on the poop, but were kept below. The heat and stifling atmosphere were inconceivable and cruel. The iron deck below presented the appearance of having been hosed — in reality it was merely the perspiration streaming off these poor persecuted captives that drenched the deck. The attention of the ship's doctor was one day called to this, and he at once forbade this inhuman confinement in future. From then onwards, batches of the prisoners were allowed on the poop at a time, so that every man could obtain at least a little fresh air a day — surely the smallest concession that could possibly be made to men living under such wretched conditions.

But notwithstanding these hardships the men seemed to be merry and bright, and showed smiling faces to their captors. They had all evidently made up their minds to keep their end up to the last, and were not to be downed by any bad news or bad treatment the Germans might give them.

The *Wolf*, of course, picked up wireless news every day, printed it, and circulated it throughout the ship in German and English. We did not, however, hear all the news that was picked up, but felt that what we did hear kept us at least a little in touch with the outside world, and we have since been able to verify that, and also to discover that we missed a great deal too. The weekly returns of submarine sinkings were regularly published, and these were followed with great interest both by the Germans and ourselves. We heard, too, some of the speeches of Mr. Lloyd George and the German Chancellors, debates in the Reichstag, and general war news, especially what was favourable to the Germans.

The accommodation provided for the married couples on the *Wolf* was situated on the port side upper deck, which corresponded in position to the promenade deck of a liner. Some "cabins" had been improvised when the first women and civilian prisoners had been captured, some had been vacated by the officers, and others had been carved out as the number of these prisoners increased. The cabins were, of course, very small—there was very little room to spare on the *Wolf*—and, at the best, makeshift contrivances, but it must be admitted that our German captors did all they could to make us as comfortable as possible under the conditions prevailing. The cabin occupied by my wife and myself was built on one of the hatches. The bunks were at different levels, and were at right angles to each other, half of one being in a dark corner. There was not much room in it even for light baggage, and not standing room for two people. The walls and ceiling were made of white painted canvas, and an electric light and fan were installed over the door. The married couples, the Australian military officers, and a few elderly civilians messed together in the officers' ward-room (presided over by a war photograph of the All Highest), quite a tiny saloon, which was placed at our disposal after the officers had finished their meals. We had breakfast at 9.15, dinner at 1.15, and supper at 7.15. The Commander of the *Wolf* was a very lonely man—he messed alone in his quarters near the bridge, and we saw very little of him, as he very rarely left his quarters and came below among his men and the prisoners.

The food on the *Wolf* was better cooked than it had been on the *Hitachi*, but there was of course no fresh food of any kind. Two or three horses had been taken from the S.S. *Matunga*—these had been shot and eaten long before. Even the potatoes we had were dried, and had to be soaked many hours before they were cooked, and even then they did not much resemble the original article; the same remark applies to the other vegetables we had. Occasionally our meals satisfied us as far as quantity went, but in the main we left the table feeling we could with ease dispose of a great deal more. This was especially the case after breakfast, which consisted of bread and jam only; and once at tiffin all we had to eat was boiled rice with cinnamon and sugar. Each cabin had a German orderly to look after and wait on its occupants, two German stewards waited on us at meals, and a Japanese steward had two or three cabins to look after and clean. The water allowance, both for drinking and washing, was very small. We had only one bottle of the former and one can of the latter between two of us; so it was impossible to wash any of our clothes.

The deck—we were only allowed the port side—was only about six feet wide, and part of this was occupied by spare spars. There were no awnings, and the sun and rain streamed right across the narrow space. Sailors and officers, and prisoners to fetch their food, were passing along this deck incessantly all day, so it can be easily imagined there was not much room for sitting about on deck chairs. On this deck, too, was the prisoners' cell, usually called the "calaboose," very rarely without an occupant, with an armed sentry on guard outside. It was not a cheerful abode, being very small and dark; and the prisoner, if his sentence were a long one, served it in instalments of a few days at a time.

We were allowed to go down to the well deck to see our friends and sit on the hatch with them during the daytime. They had their meals in the 'tween decks at different times from us, but the food provided was usually just the same. The evenings were the deadliest times of all on the *Wolf*. At dusk the order "Schiff Abblenden" resounded all through the ship, sailors came round to put tin plates over all the portholes, and from thence onward throughout the night complete darkness prevailed on deck, not a glint of light showing anywhere on the ship. It was very nasty and uncanny.

When the *Wolf* considered herself in dangerous waters, and when laying mines, even smoking was forbidden on deck. All the cabins had a device by which directly the door was open the light went out, only to be relit directly the door closed. So it was impossible for any one to leave his cabin with the door open and the light on. There was nothing to do in the evenings after the last meal, which was over before eight o'clock. We groped our way in darkness along the deck when we left the little wardroom, and there was then nowhere to sit except on the dark deck or in the dark cabins; it was so hot that the cabin doors had to be kept open, and the evenings spent on the *Wolf* were certainly very dreary. Most of us agreed with Dr. Johnson that "the man in gaol has more room, better food, and commonly better company than the man in the ship, and is in safety," and felt we would rather be in gaol on shore, for then we should be in no risk of being killed at any moment by our own people, our cells would have been larger than our cabins, and our food possibly not much worse, and our gaol would at least have been stationary and not rolling about, though it must be confessed the *Wolf* was a good sea boat.

She had been one of the Hansa line before the war, called the *Wachfels*, was about 6,000 tons, single screw, with a speed of about ten knots at the outside. She had been thoroughly adapted for her work as a raider, had four torpedo tubes and six guns (said to be 4.7), with concrete emplacements, not to mention machine and smaller guns — to be used against the prisoners if they should attempt escape, etc. — none of which could be seen by a passing ship, to which the *Wolf* looked, as she was intended to look, exactly like an innocent neutral tramp painted black. This was in itself a camouflage — she needed no other. When in action her bulwarks dropped, giving free play to her guns and torpedoes. There was telephonic communication between her bridge and every gun and every part of the ship; she carried a huge searchlight, her masts and funnel were telescopic, and she could rig an extra funnel. She carried large supplies of bombs, hand grenades, rifles and small arms; had hospitals with two doctors on board; the officers had the best and most powerful binoculars; among her crew of more than three hundred were representatives of every trade; she was thoroughly well equipped in every way, and absolutely nothing seemed to have been forgotten. There were, it was said, only three of the officers who were Imperial Navy men; the Commander, the Artillery Officer, and the Lieutenant in charge of the prisoners. All the other officers and a great many of the crew were from the German mercantile marine, who had travelled with, mixed with, and lived with Englishmen in many parts of the world. To this we undoubtedly owed the kindly treatment we received on board, treatment which was infinitely better than we expected to receive. The majority of the officers and men were certainly kindly disposed towards us. There is no doubt, however, that the fear we might be taken by a British cruiser also had something to do with this treatment, for if we had been treated badly the Germans knew they would have had cause to regret it had they been captured.

In a conversation with the Lieutenant in charge of the prisoners—who, by the way, had a Scottish mother—I remarked that it was very hard on our relations and friends not knowing what had become of us. He agreed that it was, but added it was no worse for my relations than it was for his! They did not know where he was either! "No," I replied, "but you are out doing your duty and serving your country, and when you left home your people knew they would have no news of you for many months. It is quite different with us. We are not out to be ingloriously taken prisoner, we were simply travelling on business, being compelled to do so. We are not serving our country by being caught and kept in this way, and our relatives did not expect us to disappear and send them no news of ourselves for a long time." However, he affected not to see the difference between our case and his; just as the sailors often told the prisoners aft that in case of the *Wolf* going into action it would be no worse for the prisoners than it was for the fighting crew!

We were forbidden to talk to the crew, but under cover of the darkness some of them, a great number of whom spoke English, were only too glad to speak to us. We learnt from them that the *Wolf* had been out a year; they were all very "fed up" with it all, tired of the life, tired of the sea, tired of the food, longing to get home, and longing for the war to end. They had, too, no doubts as to how it would end, and were certain that the *Wolf* would get back to Germany whenever she wished to do so. Of course we assured them that they were utterly mistaken, and that it would be absolutely impossible for the *Wolf* ever to get through the British blockade or see Germany again.

They were certain three things would bring them victory: their submarines, the defection of Russia, who would soon be made to conclude peace with Germany, and the fact that in their opinion America had entered the war too late. The submarines, too, would not allow a single transport to reach European waters!

While on the *Wolf* we heard of the great reverse to the Italian arms. We were told that half a million prisoners and thousands of guns were taken, and that there was no longer an Italian army! Germany had strafed one more country and knocked her out of the war. This made their early victory still more certain! Their spirits may be imagined when this news of Italy's disaster was received.

The interests of the *Wolf* were now, to a certain extent, identical with our own — that we should not meet an Allied cruiser. A notice was posted in some of our cabins saying that in that event the women with their husbands, and some other prisoners, would be put into boats with a white flag, "if weather and other conditions permitted." We often wondered whether they *would* permit! The other prisoners, however, viz. those under the poop and on the 'tween decks, would have had no chance of being saved. They would all have been battened down under hatches (this, indeed, was done whenever the *Wolf* sighted or captured a ship, when mines were being sown, and when gun and other drill was carried on) and armed guards with hand grenades sent among them. It made us furious to see, as we did many times, our friends being driven below by armed guards. Their fate, if the *Wolf* had gone into action, would have been too terrible to contemplate. For the lifeboats on the *Wolf* could not possibly have accommodated more than 350 souls, and it is certain no prisoners would have been among this number.

The Captain and officers of the *Wolf* must have had some very anxious moments on many occasions. When passing close to other ships, as she had done in the comparatively narrow waters of the Java Sea, all the prisoners were sent below, and we were told that the few officers and crew visible to a passing ship discarded their naval uniform and appeared in kit suitable for the officers and crew of a tramp. We also heard that on one occasion in narrow waters in the Far East the *Wolf* passed quite close to a Japanese cruiser at night. Both ships were in darkness, every man on the *Wolf* was at his station, and at the slightest sign from the cruiser the *Wolf*'s guns and torpedoes would have immediately come into action. But the *Wolf*'s good luck did not desert her, and the Japanese cruiser passed away into the night without having given any sign that she had seen the raider.

The *Wolf*, with a company of over seven hundred on board, sailed away on a south-westerly course for the next two days, and the usual routine of the ship went on, but no further gun or other drills took place. Soon after daybreak on November 10th a sailor came along and locked us all in our cabins, armed guards patrolled the deck, and a short time after an officer came to each cabin and informed us there was a steamer on the starboard side which the *Wolf* intended to capture. He told us the *Wolf* would fire on her to stop, and provided all of us with cotton-wool to insert in our ears while the guns were being fired! The Germans had had no scruples about firing on the *Hitachi*, though they could have seen there were women on board, but on this occasion they were so considerate as to give us cotton-wool for our ears, that our nerves might not be shaken—a truly German touch! We waited for the sound of the guns, but nothing happened, and in about half an hour the same officer came along and said to us, "Don't be fearful; the other ship has stopped, and there will be no firing!" Our cabin doors were unlocked, the men on the upper deck were allowed out, the ladies were requested not to show themselves on deck, and another officer ran along the deck saying "We've catched her, we've catched her; a neutral this time!"

The "catched" vessel had stopped and was lying very near the *Wolf*. The name on her stern proclaimed her to be the *Igotz Mendi*, of Bilbao, and she was flying the Spanish flag. In a short time a prize crew, with Lieutenant Rose in command, left the *Wolf* in her motor launch, and proceeded to the other ship. After they had been aboard her a few minutes, a message came back that the Spanish ship was from Delagoa Bay to Colombo with a cargo of 5,800 tons of coal for the British Admiralty authorities in Ceylon. So the Germans would not after all have to intern the *Wolf* and her prize in a neutral country—if she could reach one—at any rate from lack of coal, as we fondly imagined might have been the case. Here was just the cargo our captors wanted to annex, but the chagrin of the Germans may be imagined when they realized that they had captured this ship just three days too late to save the *Hitachi*. Here was a ship with ample coal which, had it been captured a few days before, would have enabled the Germans to save the *Hitachi* and take her as a prize to Germany, with all of us on board as prisoners, as they had always desired to do. Other German raiders had occasionally been able to do so with one or two of their prizes. Had the *Hitachi* arrived in Germany, she would have been rechristened the *Luchs*, the name of a former German war vessel with which the Prize Captain had had associations.

The *Igotz Mendi* had left Lourenço Marques on November 5th, and was due at Colombo on the 22nd. Before 9 a.m. on the morning of the capture both ships had turned about, the prize now being in command of the Germans, and were going back on the course the *Wolf* had followed since the destruction of the *Hitachi*. Discussion was rife among the prisoners as to what would be done with the new capture, and whether the Commander of the *Wolf* would redeem his promise to transfer the married couples to the "next ship caught."

Chapter VI. Another Prize – Our Future Home

The two ships steamed along in company for the next three days, usually stopping towards sunset for communications and sending orders. On Sunday, the 11th, we were invited to a band performance on the well deck forward. It was quite a good one. The first mate came along and jokingly said to us, "What more can you want? We give you a free passage, free food, and even free music." I replied, "We only want one more thing free." "What is that?" he asked. "Freedom," I answered. "Ah!" he said, smiling, "I am afraid you must wait for that a little time."

I had asked him earlier in the day if he would allow us the use of a room and a piano for a short time in the afternoon, so that we could keep up our custom of singing a few hymns on Sunday. Later on, he told me we might, with the permission of the officers, have their wardroom for half an hour. The officers and he had kindly agreed to this, a concession we much appreciated, and the little wardroom was crowded indeed on that occasion.

At daybreak on the 13th both ships arrived at the Nazareth Bank, and before 9 a.m. were lashed together. On such occasions the *Wolf* never dropped anchor, for she might have to be up and away at the slightest warning; the prize ship was always the one to drop anchor. On the previous Tuesday the *Wolf* had been lashed alongside the *Hitachi*; here, on this Tuesday, was the *Wolf* lashed alongside another captured ship in the very same place! Again the daring and coolness of our captors amazed us. Coaling the *Wolf* from the *Igotz Mendi* at once began, and a wireless installation was immediately rigged up by the Germans on the Spanish ship. Coaling proceeded all that day, and the German officers and crews on both ships were very busy. The prisoners aft were also very busy, catching fish over the side. No sooner had the ships stopped than lines were dropped overboard and many fine fish were caught. The prisoners aft wore very little clothing and often no head-gear at all, though we were in the tropics, where we had always thought a sun-helmet was a *sine qua non*. But the prisoners got on quite well without one.

On the morning of the 14th, just six weeks after our capture, orders were given to the married couples on the *Wolf* to get their light baggage ready at once for transference to the Spanish ship, as she and the *Wolf* might have to separate at any moment.

Our heavy baggage would be transferred if time allowed. We did not understand at the time why the Germans were so considerate to us in the matter of baggage, but later on, a great deal later on, light dawned on us! It is doubtful, to say the least of it, if we should have been allowed to keep our baggage if we should be taken to Germany, a possibility that was always present in our minds. We know now that it always was the intention of the Germans to take us to Germany, and that being the case, it would be just as simple to relieve us of our luggage when we got there as to deprive us of it while we were *en route*.

Evidently something was in the air; some wireless message had been picked up, as the seaplane was being brought up from the 'tween decks and assembled at great haste on the well deck. The *Wölfchen* went up about 4.20 and returned about 5.30, and in the interval our heavy baggage had been brought up from the *Wolf*'s hold ready to be transferred to the *Igotz Mendi*.

At dusk that evening the married people were transferred to the Spanish ship. We felt very sad at leaving our *Hitachi* and other friends on the *Wolf*, and feared that whatever might happen to us, they would never be free. For ourselves, too, the prospect was not a very pleasing one. The whole ship was smothered in coal-dust, the saloon was almost pitch-dark, as awnings had been hung over all the ports, the atmosphere was stifling, the cabins we were to occupy were still littered with the belongings of their former occupants, and the outlook was certainly very dreary. To make things worse a thick drizzle came on, converting the coal-dust on deck into an evil, black, muddy ooze.

The next morning we were still alongside the *Wolf*, and remained there till the morning of the 17th, our heavy baggage being transhipped in the interval. There had also been transferred the Colonel of the A.A.M.C. already mentioned, and three other men—including the second mate of one ship previously captured—who were in ill-health. One of the *Hitachi* prisoners, a man over military age, who had come on board at Colombo straight from hospital, and was going for a health voyage to South Africa, had been told in the morning that he was to be transferred to the Spanish ship. But later on, much to the regret of every one, it was found that the Germans would not release him. A German officer came up to him and said in my hearing, "Were you not told this morning that you were to go on the *Igotz Mendi*?" "Yes," he replied. "Well," said the officer, "you're not to." Comment on the brutal manner of this remark is unnecessary.

The message the seaplane had brought back had evidently been a reassuring one, and we heard a long time afterwards that the *Wolf* had picked up a wireless from a Japanese cruiser, presumably looking for the *Hitachi*, only thirty miles away. Hence the alarm! Unfortunately for us, if this report were true, the cruiser did not turn aside to look in the most obvious place where a ship like the *Wolf* would hide, so once more the *Wolf* was safe.

If only there had been a couple of cruisers disguised, like the *Wolf*, as tramps, each one carrying a seaplane or two, in each ocean free from submarine attentions, the *Wolf* could have been seen and her career brought to an end long before. The same end would probably have been attained on this occasion if a wireless message had been sent from Delagoa Bay to Colombo saying that the *Igotz Mendi* had left the former port for the latter with 5,000 tons of coal on board. The strong wireless installation on the *Wolf*, which picked up every message within a large radius, but of course never sent any, would have picked up this message, and the *Wolf* would probably have risen to the bait, with the result that she could have been caught by an armed vessel sent in search of her on that track. For it must have been known that a raider was out in those waters, as the disappearance of the *Hitachi* could only have been due to the presence of one.

Coaling proceeded without cessation till the morning of the 17th, when the *Wolf* moved off a short distance. Passengers on mail-boats familiar with the process of coaling ship at Port Said, Colombo, or any other port, can imagine the condition of these ships, after three or four days' incessant coaling day and night.

The appearance of the *Igotz Mendi* was meanwhile undergoing another change. When captured she was painted white and had a buff funnel with her company's distinguishing mark. She was now painted the Allied grey colour, and when her sides and funnel had been transformed the two ships sailed away, and on the evening of the 17th, after final orders and instructions had been given, parted company. For some days after this, painting was the order of the day on the Spanish ship, which was now grey on every part visible.

The Captain of the Spanish ship was now relieved of his duties—and also of his cabin, which the German Captain had annexed, leaving the owner thereof the chartroom to sleep in—and was naturally very chagrined at the course events had taken, especially as he said he had been informed by the Consul at Lourenço Marques that the course between there and Colombo was quite clear, and had not even been informed of the disappearance of the *Hitachi*, though she had been overdue at Delagoa Bay about a month. Consequently he had been showing his navigation lights at sea, and without them the *Wolf* would probably not have seen him, as it was about 1 a.m. when the *Wolf* picked him up.

The remaining Spanish officers took their watch on the bridge, always with a member of the prize crew in attendance; the Spanish engineers remained in charge of the engine-room, again with a German always present; and the Spanish crew remained on duty as before. There was a prize crew of nine Germans on board; the Captain, Lieutenant Rose, who had also been in charge of the *Hitachi* after her capture, and the First Officer, who had also filled that post on the *Hitachi*, being the only officers. Lieutenant Rose spoke Spanish in addition to English and French, and the Spanish Captain also spoke very good English. Some of the Spanish officers also spoke English, but the knowledge of it was not so general as it was on the *Wolf*, where every officer we met spoke our language, and most of the prize crew spoke quite enough to get on with.

The Spanish Captain, a charming gentleman, and in appearance anything but a seafaring man, was, however, frankly puzzled by some current English slang. One of the passenger prisoners—the hero of the kerosene porridge—was known among us as the "hot-air merchant." This was simple enough, but when we said he also suffered from cold feet, the Spanish Captain admitted defeat. Such a contradictory combination seemed inconceivable. "If a man were full of hot air, how could he have cold feet?" he said. Lieutenant Rose, however, was *au fait* with the latest English slang, and always used it correctly.

The *Igotz Mendi*, 4,600 tons, had been completed in 1916, and was a ship admirably fitted for her purpose, which, however, was not that of carrying passengers. Ordinarily she was a collier, or carried iron ore. Her decks were of iron, scorchingly hot in the tropics and icy cold in northern latitudes. There was no place sheltered from the sun in which to sit on the small deck space, and the small awnings which were spasmodically rigged up were quite insufficient for the purpose. There were now twenty-one "passenger" prisoners on board, including the Japanese stewardess, and five Asiatics. There were no cabins except those provided for the officers, who generously gave them up to the married couples on board, the officers taking quarters much more crowded and much less desirable. The Germans installed a small electric fan, taken from the *Hitachi*, in each cabin, and also one in the saloon. The cabins were quite suitable for one occupant each, but very cramped for two; the one occupied by my wife and myself being only seven and a half feet square. Each contained one bunk and one settee, the latter being a sleeping-place far from comfortable, as it was only five and a half feet long by about twenty inches wide, the bunk being the same width, but longer, and the floor space was very narrow and restricted. Our light baggage had to be kept on the bunk all day, being deposited on the washstand and floor every night. Our first duty every morning was to replace the baggage on the bunk, so that we could have room to stand on the floor! There were four cabins, two on each side of a narrow alley-way about two feet wide, while one married couple occupied the Chief Engineer's cabin further aft on the starboard side, quite a roomy apartment. The port cabin opposite to it was occupied by an old Mauritius-Indian woman and her little granddaughter (who was often very naughty and got many "lickings" from her grandmother, whom she frequently implored the Captain to throw overboard), the Japanese stewardess, the Australian stewardess already mentioned, and a coloured man going to South Africa with his Chinese wife. Rather crowded quarters, not to mention somewhat unseemly conditions! The Asiatic passengers had been "intermediate" passengers on the *Hitachi*, i.e. between the second-class and deck passengers. The four men above mentioned occupied a space under the poop—it could not be dignified with the name of cabin. It was very small, only one occupant could dress at a time, and immediately in front of it was a reeking pigsty with three full-sized occupants. The passage to it from the saloon on the upper deck was often a perilous one in rough weather and on dark nights, for there was never any light showing on board at night during the whole cruise. Occasionally a lifeline was rigged along the well deck to the poop quarters, a by no means unnecessary precaution. The prize crew had quarters on the starboard side under the poop; they were exceedingly small, cramped, and in every way inconvenient and uncomfortable. Our heavy baggage was also stored under the poop.

This, then, was to be our home, possibly for the next few months. We did not know for how long, but we regarded the prospect with a certain amount of equanimity, as the ship was unarmed, and we knew we should not be fired on by a hostile cruiser, as might have been the case if we had remained on the *Wolf*.

When we arrived on the Spanish boat we were served with meals at the same time to which the Spanish officers had been accustomed, i.e. breakfast at 9 and supper at 4, but these times were soon afterwards changed to breakfast at 8.30, tiffin 12.30, and supper 5.30. We were lucky to get fresh food for some days. But this soon came to an end, though the stock of muscatels, a quince preserve—called membrillo—and Spanish wine lasted very much longer. It would have lasted much longer still but for the stupidity of the German sailor who "managed" the canteen. He allowed stores to be eaten in plenty while there were any, instead of arranging to spread their consumption over a much longer period.

There was on board a certain amount of live stock; some chickens, which seemed to thrive quite well on coal-dust, and a couple of cows, each of which had a calf born on board; these all met the usual fate of such things on appropriate occasions. There were also a few cats and kittens, which later on were joined by a couple of mongrel dachshund pups born on the *Wolf*. The Spanish carpenter had a sporting hen, which had some lively scraps with the dogs, the latter always coming off second best.

For many days after we parted company with the *Wolf* we ambled and dawdled through the sea on a south-westerly course, sometimes going back on our tracks for half a day, sometimes stopping altogether for an hour or two, sometimes for half a day, sometimes for a whole day. The monotony of this performance was deadly beyond words. On one of these days the Captain offered to land us at Mauritius on the following morning and give himself up with the crew and ship if we could raise £100,000 for him. Unfortunately, we couldn't!

On the afternoon of the 23rd the Germans became very agitated at the sight of smoke on the horizon. At first we all thought it was the *Wolf*, but before long we could see two columns of smoke, evidently coming from two steamers travelling together. The prisoners then became very agitated also, as help might be at hand. But the Germans at once changed the course, and manœuvred at full speed in such a way that we soon got out of sight of the smoke, when we resumed our original course again, after having boxed the compass more than once, and the German Captain came down from the bridge and told us there was no relief for us yet. We all felt that if the *Hitachi* had only avoided distant smoke as the German Captain had done we need never have made the acquaintance of the *Wolf*.

On the 24th we again met the *Wolf* in the evening. Whenever the *Wolf* had an appointment to meet her prize at a certain time and place, the prize always hoisted recognition signals directly she saw the *Wolf* on the horizon. These were made of wicker, and varied in shape on different occasions.

We were now well to the south of Africa, in the roaring forties, and we saw many schools of whales, and albatrosses accompanied us for many days. A Spanish officer shot one one day — we told him this would bring us bad luck, as the souls of lost sea captains are said to inhabit these majestic birds. And one day we saw a dead whale floating along not far from the ship — it was smothered with a huge flock of seabirds, gorging themselves on it. By December 1st we had begun to steer north-west, and on the 3rd the Captain informed us we were the nearest we should ever be to Cape Town, the port to which I had set out. On this morning the Captain said to me, "Mr. Trayes, didn't you say you were going to Cape Town?" "Yes," I replied. "Come out on deck with me," he answered. I went with him. He took my arm, and said, "There it is," pointing in its direction. We were then 150 miles off! We met the *Wolf* again on the 5th, and travelled in her company during the remainder of that day and the next two, stopping as usual for communication and the sending of stores to us in the evenings just before sunset. Often when the ship stopped Lieutenant Rose would go aboard the *Wolf*, another Lieutenant boarding us and remaining in charge during his absence. The *Wolf* on this occasion told us she had sunk the American sailing vessel *John H. Kirby* from America to East London with a cargo of four hundred motor-cars on board, when two days from her destination, the officers and crew being taken on board the *Wolf*. Many people in South Africa would have to dispense with their motor joy-rides at Christmas in consequence.

The evening of December 7th was the last occasion we saw the *Wolf* for many days. The two ships now shaped a course for the Brazilian Island of Trinidad, where it was understood the *Wolf* would coal from her prize, and with her spend the Christmas holidays.

Chapter VII. Christmas on the „Igotz Mendi"

It must not be supposed that the life of the prisoners on the *Igotz Mendi* in any way approximated to that of passengers on an ordinary passenger ship. To begin with, there were no ship's servants to wait on us with the exception of the Spanish steward, a youth who "waited" at table and excelled in breaking ship's crockery. Often he poured the coffee over us, or into our pockets, instead of into our cups, and on one occasion, during a heavier roll than usual, he fell down in the middle of the saloon while carrying a tureen full of soup. It went flying over the saloon and some of its occupants, so our soup ration was short that day.

If the cabins were to be kept clean, we had to do it ourselves. Every morning saw the occupants sweeping out and cleaning up their cabins, as no ship's servant ever entered them. The water supply was very limited, and had to be fetched by ourselves — no matter what the weather — sometimes from the fore peak and sometimes from a pump near the ship's galley. Washing water and drinking water were served out twice a day, at 8 a.m. and 4 p.m., an ordinary water-can being the allowance of the former, and a water-bottle that of the latter. The supply of washing water was very inadequate, and no hot water was ever available. After washing ourselves, we had to wash our clothes in the same water — for there was of course no laundry on board — and then the cabin floor after that. By this time the water was mud. It was impossible to have a proper bath all the time we were on board, for there was no water supply in the bathroom, and it was kept in an extremely dirty condition. "Laundry work" was usually done by the prisoners after breakfast, and lines were rigged on any available part of the ship to dry the clothes. It was a sight for the gods to see the military officers presiding at their washtubs on deck, and then hanging out their washing. On fine days with a big wash the array of drying garments in various parts of the ship was quite imposing.

My wife managed to borrow some irons from the Australian stewardess, which she heated on the stove in the cook's galley. With these she ironed her blouses and my shirts and soft collars, while I helped with the hankeys. The ironing space was not ideal, being the cover, about twenty inches square, of the cabin washstand. But the result was highly creditable!

The saloon, about eighteen feet square, in which all the meals were served in two sittings, was very rarely clean, and the habits of the Captain's mongrel pup, born on the *Wolf*, did not improve matters. *Something* connected with the expedition had to be called "Luchs," so, failing the *Hitachi*, the pup rejoiced in this name, and as he frequently made the saloon so exclusively his own, it was often appropriately named the "Salon de luxe." Poor Luchs! Every man's hand, or rather foot—with the exception of the Captain's—was against him (when the Captain was not looking!) on account of his reprehensible behaviour. Many a sly kick was aimed at him, and when a yelp assured us that the blow had struck home, one of us would exclaim, "Hooray for our side!"; "our side" being all who suffered from his bad conduct. The table "appointments" were often disgusting. The tablecloth was filthy after the first meal or so, thanks to the rolling of the ship and consequent upsetting of soup, tea, and coffee, but was only changed twice, sometimes only once, a week. Cups were used without saucers, and spoons gradually disappeared, so that towards the end one had to suffice between four or five persons.

The ship, generally speaking, was filthy—she was never properly clean. I remember on one occasion a large bottle of castor-oil was smashed just outside the saloon door. The stuff remained there for hours before being cleaned up. The crew certainly was not large, but a great deal more could have been done in the direction of keeping the ship clean, and her condition was never a credit to her Captain. This was a surprise to those of us who had previously travelled on German ships.

We got thoroughly sick of the food provided, but the German officers and crew had just the same. The *Hitachi* had been carrying ten thousand cases of Japanese canned crab to England. A great part of this was saved, and divided between the *Wolf* and her prize. None of us ever want to see or hear of this commodity again; we were fed on it till most of us loathed it, but as there was nothing else to eat when it was served, we perforce had to eat that or dry bread, and several of us chose the latter. How we groaned when we saw any more crab being brought over from the *Wolf!* Bully beef, every variety of bean, dried vegetables, dried fish that audibly announced its advent to the table, bean soup, and pea soup (maggot soup would often have been a more correct description), we got just as sick of, till, long before the end, all the food served nauseated us. Tea, sometimes made in a coffee-pot, sometimes even with salt water, was the usual hot drink provided, but coffee was for some time available once a day. We owe a great debt to one of our fellow-prisoners, a ship's cook, captured from one of the other ships, who in return for his offer to work as baker was promised his liberty, which fortunately he has now secured, though no thanks to the Germans. He baked, under the most difficult conditions, extraordinarily good bread, and over and over again we should have gone without food but for this. We were often very hungry, for there was nothing to eat between "supper" at 5.30 and breakfast next morning at 8.30. The Captain had given each lady a large box of biscuits from the *Hitachi*, and my wife and I used to eat a quarter of a biscuit each before turning in for the night. We could not afford more—the box might have to last us for many months.

We could not buy much on board. The only thing of which there seemed to be plenty was whisky, all stolen from the captured ships. When our ship ran short of this, more was sent over from the *Wolf*. We could buy this at reasonable rates, but the supply was always supposed to be rationed. Soap and toilet requisites became very scarce or failed altogether as time went on. We could buy an infinitesimal piece of stolen toilet soap for a not infinitesimal price, and were rationed as to washing soap and matches. The currency on board was a very mixed one, consisting of Japanese yen, both in silver and paper money, English, Spanish, and German silver, and German canteen tokens—all marked S.M.S. *Victoria Louise*—ranging in value from 2 marks to 5 pfennig.

Mention has been made of the ship's rolling. Her capacity for this was incredible—in the smoothest sea, whether stopped or under steam, she rolled heavily from side to side, and caused great discomfort, inconvenience, and often alarm to all on board. The remark, "The Mendi roll, fresh every day for every meal, for breakfast, dinner, and tea," was made by some one at almost every mealtime, as we clutched at our food, gliding or jumping from end to end of the saloon table, accompanied by the smashing of crockery and upsetting of liquids and soup. We were hardly ever able to sit still at mealtimes, but were always rocking and rolling about, usually with our plates in our hands, as leaving them on the table meant we might lose the contents. Even the Captain was astonished at the rolling of the ship, as he well might have been, when one night he, in common with most of us, was flung out of his berth. No ship ever rolled like it—the bath in the bathroom even got loose and slid about in its socket, adding to the great din on board.

As may be imagined, there was not much to do on board. The few books we had between us were passed round and read over and over again. Some were also sent over from the *Wolf* for us. Card games of various kinds also helped to pass the time, and the Captain and some of the prisoners held a "poker school" morning, afternoon, and evening in the saloon. But time, nevertheless, dragged very heavily. Some of us had occasionally to carry our mattresses and beds out on to the deck, to hunt for bugs, which were very numerous in some cabins. But the pastime was hardly one to be recommended! And, it must regretfully be admitted, we all managed to do nothing quite comfortably!

We were at liberty to go practically where we liked on board, but we were never able to get far away from the German sailors, who always appeared to be listening to our conversation, no matter where we were. As on the *Wolf*, they were sometimes caught spying on us, and listening at the portholes or ventilators of our cabins.

We next picked up the *Wolf* on the afternoon of December 19th, and heard that since we had last seen her she had sunk a French sailing vessel, the *Maréchal Davout*, loaded with grain for Europe. The *Wolf* usually sent us over a budget of wireless news when she had been away from us any length of time. I remember an item of news on one occasion, in which Mr. Lloyd George in a speech said we were getting on the track of the submarines and that we had sunk five in one day. This gave great mirth to the Germans, who naturally refused to believe it—they said they had lost only a dozen since the war began! On one occasion the Captain informed us of a "great British victory. Joy-bells are ringing all over England. The British have captured a trench and have advanced ten yards!" This was the victory at Cambrai!

The two ships proceeded on parallel courses for Trinidad, but about 8 p.m. both ships turned sharply round and doubled on their tracks, proceeding on a south-easterly course at full speed. We learnt the reason for this the next day. German raiders had previously coaled and hidden at Trinidad; but Brazil was now in the war, so that hole was stopped, and the *Wolf* had intercepted a wireless from the Commander of a Brazilian cruiser to the garrison on Trinidad. Hence her rapid flight! But for that wireless message, the *Wolf* would have walked right into the trap, and we should have been free within twelve hours from the time the *Wolf* picked up the message.

Once again wireless had been our undoing. The *Hitachi* had wirelessed the hour of her arrival at and departure from Singapore and Colombo; the *Wolf*, of course, had picked up the messages and was ready waiting for her. One other ship, if not more, was caught in just the same way. The *Matunga* had wirelessed, not even in code, her departure, with the nature of her cargo, from Sydney to New Guinea, and she wirelessed again when within a few hours of her destination. The *Wolf* waited for her, informed her that she had on board just the cargo the *Wolf* needed, captured, and afterwards sunk her. The *Wolf*'s success in capturing ships and evading hostile cruisers was certainly due to her intercepting apparently indiscriminate wirelessing between ships, and between ships and shore—at one time in the Indian Ocean the *Wolf* was picking up news in four languages—and to her seaplane, which enabled her to scout thoroughly and to spot an enemy ship long before she could have been seen by the enemy. Thus the *Wolf*'s procedure when hunting for her prey was simplicity itself. Even without wireless her seaplane was of enormous assistance to her. If her "bird" had revealed the presence of a ship more heavily armed than the *Wolf* chose to tackle, she could easily make herself scarce, while if the ship seen was not at all, or but lightly armed, all that the *Wolf* had to do was to wait for her on the course she was taking.

Soon after leaving the Indian Ocean the seaplane had been taken to pieces and placed in the 'tween decks, so that if the *Wolf* had been seen by another steamer, her possession of a seaplane would not have been revealed.

The two ships proceeded on their new course at full speed for the next two days. On the 21st they slowed down, hoping to coal in the open sea. The next day both ships stopped, but the condition of the sea would not admit of coaling; we were then said to be about 700 miles E. of Monte Video. It was a great disappointment to the Germans that they were prevented from coaling and spending their Christmas under the shelter of Trinidad, but it became quite clear that all the holes for German raiders in this part of the ocean had now been stopped, and that they would have to coal in the open sea or not at all. Some of us thought the Germans might go back to Tristan da Cunha, or even to Gough Island—both British possessions in the South Atlantic—but the Germans would not risk this. Even St. Helena was mentioned as a possible coaling place, but the Germans said that was impracticable, as it would mean an attack on an unfortified place: as if this would have been a new procedure for German armed forces! The fact that they knew St. Helena to be fortified probably had a great deal more to do with their decision not to proceed there!

But the disappointment about Trinidad was mitigated by other wireless news received. The Commander of the *Wolf* called all his men together and harangued them to the effect that the latest news was that Russia and Roumania were now out of the war, having given in to Germany, that the Italian disasters had knocked Italy out in addition, that the war would certainly be over in six months, and that the *Wolf* would then go home in safety to a victorious, grateful, and appreciative Fatherland. Some such spur as this was very necessary to the men, who were getting very discontented with the length of the cruise and conditions prevailing, notably the monotony of the cruise and threatened shortage of food and drink and tobacco.

(The *Wolf* had brought out from Germany enormous stores of provisions for the cruise, which was expected to last about a year. In fact, her cargo from Germany consisted of coal, stores, ammunition, and mines only. She replenished her stores solely from the prizes she took.)

The Germans were thoroughly confident of victory, and very cock-a-hoop now that Russia and Roumania were knocked out, and Italy, so they said, so thoroughly defeated as to be quite a negligible factor in the future. Our enemies could not conceal their joy at the good news their wireless brought them. They crowed over us, and at mealtimes the Captain explained how, with the "three and a half millions" of their troops released from the Russian fronts, defeat for the Allies was inevitable in a very few months. A German victory was now as sure as to-morrow's sunrise. "But, of course," he said, "there will first be an armistice to discuss terms." We asked him what he meant by an armistice. He replied that the troops on the front would cease fighting. "And your submarines?" we asked. "Oh! they will go on with their work," he replied. "Why should they stop?" Why, indeed? It was to be a *German* armistice, graciously permitted by our enemies, in which they were to continue the use of a deadly weapon, but we were to lay down our arms! Generally speaking, however, we refused to be drawn into discussion of the war, its causes and issues. The enemy was "top dog" for the time being, we were in his power: we did not know what was in store for us; we did not wish to prejudice any chances we might have, and it would not pay to lose our tempers or be indiscreet.

Christmas Eve was still too rough for the ships to tie up alongside, and our Christmas the next day was the reverse of merry. The Germans had held a Christmas service on the *Wolf* on Christmas Eve, and sounds of the band and singing were wafted to us over the waters. We could have no music on the *Igotz Mendi*, as we had no piano, but our friends on the *Wolf*, so we heard afterwards, gathered together in the 'tween decks and joined in some Christmas music.

I went out on deck early on Christmas morning, and there met the Spanish Chief Mate chewing a bun. He asked me to share half with him—a great sacrifice! Such was the commencement of our Christmas festivities. Later in the morning the Spanish Captain regaled the ladies with some choice brand of Spanish wine, and offered first-class cigars to the men prisoners (rather better than the "Stinkadoros" sometimes offered us by the crew), German officers on the ships exchanged visits, and we all tried to feel the day was not quite ordinary.

Our thoughts and wishes on this sad Christmas Day turned to our friends and relations at home who would be mourning us as dead, and may perhaps be "better imagined than described," and with the bad news from the various seats of war we all felt fairly blue.

The German officers had a great feast and a jolly time on the *Wolf*. One cow and three pigs had been killed for the Christmas feast, but they did not go far between eight hundred people. The day before we had been served with some of the "in'ards," or, as the American said, the "machinery" of the poor beasts cut up into small pieces, even the lungs being used. Some of us turned up our noses at this, but the Captain assured us that if we ever *did* get to America or England we should find that the U boats had reduced our countries to such straits that even such "machinery" would be welcome food!

With Christmas Day came to an end for us a quarter of a year's captivity, and all the prisoners, at least, were glad when the dismal farce of Christmas under such conditions was over.

"This is the life," said the German sailor who supplied us with water twice daily. He was a very hardworked member of the prize crew, doing all sorts of odd jobs and always willing to help, and was said to be the black sheep of a high German family, which numbered among its members officers holding high commands in the German army and navy. If he thought it "was the life," we didn't!

The Germans showed us the "Second Christmas Annual of the *Wolf*." It was very well got up, with well-drawn and clever illustrations of their exploits, and caricatures of some of their officers and prisoners. One picture illustrated the *Wolf* running the blockade on her outward voyage. If the picture represented anything like the truth, she must have got through by the very skin of her teeth! The covers of both "Annuals" were very striking and very cleverly done.

The weather on Boxing Day was only a little more favourable than that on Christmas Day, but the Germans decided to wait no longer to coal the *Wolf*. They had previously conveyed water to our ship from the *Wolf* in boats. The same method of transferring coal was discussed, but that idea was abandoned. At 5 p.m. she tied up alongside us. She bumped into us with considerable force when she came up, and not many of us on board the *Igotz Mendi* will ever forget that night of terror. Both ships were rolling heavily, and repeatedly bumping into each other, each ship quivering from end to end, and the funnel of the *Igotz Mendi* was visibly shaking at every fresh collision. Sleep was impossible for any one on our boat; in fact, many feared to turn in at all, as they thought some of the plates of the boats might be stove in. We wandered about from cabin to deck, and from deck to cabin, trying in vain to get to sleep. The Spanish Chief Engineer came to us on the deck about 4 a.m. and did his best in his broken English to assure us everything was all right. "Go sleep tranquil," he said: "I see this ship built—very strong." But the whole performance was a horrid nightmare.

The next day was no better, but rather worse. About 6 p.m. there was a great crash, which alarmed all; it was due to the *Wolf* crashing into and completely smashing part of the bridge of our ship. This was enough for the Germans. They decided to suspend operations, and at 7 p.m. the *Wolf* sheered off, only just narrowly escaping cutting off the poop of the *Igotz Mendi* in the process. She had coaled six hundred tons in twenty-five hours, her decks, torpedo tubes, and guns being buried under great mounds of coal, as all hands were busy in the transference of coal from her prize to the *Wolf*. Shifting the coal to her bunkers had to be done after the ships had separated. If by good luck an Allied cruiser had appeared at this time, the *Wolf* would have been an easy prey. The coaling process had severely damaged the *Wolf*, many of whose plates were badly dented. We had lost eighteen large fenders between the ships, and the *Wolf* was leaking to the extent of twelve tons an hour. The *Igotz Mendi* had come off better. None of her plates were dented, she was making no water, and the only visible signs of damage to her were many twisted and bent stanchions on the port side that met the *Wolf*.

We had been allowed to send letters for Christmas — censored, of course, by the Germans — to our *Hitachi* friends on the *Wolf*, and when the two ships were alongside we were allowed to speak to them, though conversation under such conditions was very difficult, as one minute our friends would be several feet above us and the next below us with the rolling of the ships; and the noise of the coaling, shouting of orders, and roaring of the water between the ships was deafening. There did not seem much point in censoring letters, as the prisoners on the *Igotz Mendi* and the *Wolf* were allowed to talk to each other a day or so after the letters were sent, and although a German sentry was on guard while these conversations were going on, it was possible for the prisoners to say what they liked to each other, as the sentry could only have caught an occasional word or two.

I have since been asked why the prisoners and Spaniards on the Spanish ship did not attack the prize crew and seize the ship when we were not in company with the *Wolf*. It sounds quite simple, but it must be remembered that although the prize crew was certainly a small one, they were well supplied with arms, bombs, and hand grenades, while the prisoners and Spaniards had no arms at all, as they had all been taken away by the Germans. Further, an attack of this kind would have been far worse than useless unless its absolute success could have been definitely assured. There were very few young and able men among the prisoners, while the German prize crew were all picked men, young and powerful. The working crew of the ship was composed of Spaniards and other neutrals, including a Greek and a Chilian. It would have been absolutely necessary to have secured the allegiance and support of every one of these. The plan of seizing the ship, which sounds so simple, was discussed among us many a time, but it was in reality quite impracticable. What would our fate have been if we had tried—and failed? And what of the women and children on board?

Chapter VIII. Rumours and Plans

We had been encouraged by the Germans to think—they had in fact definitely told us—that the *Igotz Mendi* with us on board was to be sent to Spain when the Germans released her. This news greatly rejoiced the Spaniards, who had naturally become very depressed, more especially as they knew that if no news were received of them for six weeks after the date on which they were due at Colombo a requiem mass would, according to Spanish custom, be said for them at their churches at home.

On December 29th, all of which and the previous day, together with many succeeding days, were spent in transferring our cargo coal to our bunkers, the Germans on our ship and on the *Wolf* ostentatiously bade each other good-bye, and letters from prisoners on the *Wolf* were brought to us to post in Spain when we landed. The idea of the *Wolf* remaining out till the war was over in six months was abandoned, and we were told the *Wolf* would now go home to Germany. Why we were told this—the first time we had been informed of the *Wolf*'s plans—we never knew, except that it might have been an excuse to keep dragging us over the seas, for the *Wolf* would never have allowed us to get ashore before she reached Germany. Now that we know that the Germans always intended taking us to Germany, it is obvious that it was quite immaterial to them if they told us their plans. They wished to keep us, and having told us of their future plans, it is plain they could not afford to release us.

But at that time we really began to think we were going to be landed in Spain, and the news raised the spirits of all of us. I remember Lieutenant Rose telling the American Captain one day during a meal that he could now keep his eyes directed to a Spanish port! Those who had been learning Spanish before now did so with redoubled energy, and some of us even marked out on a pocket atlas our railway route from Bilbao or Cadiz—for the Spanish Captain thought it most likely we should be landed at one of those ports—through Spain and France. We even got information from the Spaniards as to hotels, and railways, and sights to see in Spain. It seemed as if the end of our cruise, with our freedom, were really in sight, especially as the Captain had told some of us on December 16th that in six weeks our captivity would be over. Some of us, however, still inclined to the belief that the Germans would release the ship and order her back to Java or Colombo or Calcutta; while others believed we should ultimately be landed in Dutch Guiana or Mexico, two of the few neutral countries left.

On the last day of the year a rumour went round the ship that we should be taken far north—about 60° N.—to a point from which the *Wolf* could get to Germany before we could reach Spain. That, in the opinion of most of us, put an end to the prospect of landing in Spain. The Germans would run no risks of our giving information about the *Wolf*. But this scheme would have left uneliminated one very important risk. After the ships would have separated, there was still a chance of the prize being intercepted by an Allied cruiser before the *Wolf* got home, and if that had happened the *Wolf*'s goose would have been cooked indeed. So that Spain looked very improbable. I approached the Captain on the last day of the year and spoke to him on the point. He confirmed the rumour, and said we should be sent back and landed at a Spanish island, most probably Las Palmas. I made a vigorous, though I knew it would be quite a useless, protest against this scheme. I pointed out that the ship, which by then would be almost empty, was not a suitable one in which to carry women and children into the North Atlantic in mid-winter gales, and that people who had spent many years in the tropics would not be able to stand such weather, unprovided as they were with winter clothing (although the Commander of the *Wolf* had certainly sent over some rolls of flannelette—stolen from the *Hitachi*—for the ladies to make themselves warm garments!). Also that in case of distress we could call for no help, as our wireless would only receive and not send messages. The Captain brushed these complaints aside, saying the ship was in good trim and could stand any weather, that it would only be intensely cold on a very few days, that arrangements would be made that we should suffer as little from the cold as possible, and that there was very little likelihood of our being in distress.

I then pointed out to him that our own Government prohibited our women from travelling through the submarine zone at all, but that he proposed to send them through it twice and to give us a double dose of the North Atlantic at the very worst time of the year. He replied that going north we should go nowhere near the submarine zone, that he was just as anxious to avoid submarines as we were, and that when we parted far up in the North Atlantic, the *Igotz Mendi* would be given a "submarine pass," guaranteeing her safety from attack by the U boats, and special lights to burn at nights. I replied that I failed to see the use of a "submarine pass," as U boats torpedoed at sight, and would not trouble to ask for a pass. He replied by asking me if I had ever heard of a neutral boat being torpedoed without warning. I answered that I had heard of such being done many times, and reminded him that the *Igotz Mendi* was painted the Allied grey colour and therefore would not be recognized as a neutral, but regarded by the U boats as an enemy ship. The Captain became very angry—the only time he ever lost his temper with me—and ended the interview by saying that he was carrying out the orders of the *Wolf's* Commander, and had no choice but to obey. This was undoubtedly true, and though Lieutenant Rose told us many lies concerning our destination, we always felt he was acting in accordance with instructions from his senior officer in so doing. We all recognized that we were lucky in that he, and not the Commander of the *Wolf* or any other officer of the Imperial Navy, was in charge of us. He admitted, however, that it was particularly hard luck on my wife and myself being captured like this, just as we had retired from a long period of work and residence in the Far East. This news of the *Wolf's* intentions angered us all, and we all felt that there was very little chance of ever seeing land again, unless an Allied cruiser came to our aid. We regarded this plan of the Germans as a deliberate one to sink us and the ship when they had got all they wanted out of her, and I told the Captain that my wife and I would prefer to be shot that day rather than face such a prospect of absolute misery, with every chance of death alone putting an end to it.

New Year's Day! With the dawn of 1918 we looked back on the last few months of its predecessor and what they had meant and brought to us all. What would the New Year bring forth? Liberty, or continued captivity; life, or death at sea? On New Year's morning we wished each other good luck and a Happy New Year, but with the news of our captors' intentions given us on the preceding day our prospects were the reverse of rosy.

The two ships had parted on the evening of the 30th, both going north, and we did not see the *Wolf* again till the morning of January 4th. She was then seen to be overhauling a ship on the horizon. We followed at a short distance, and before long saw a ship in full sail. The *Wolf* approached her, spoke to her, and, to our intense astonishment, released her. It seemed too good to be true that the *Wolf* would leave any ship she met quite unmolested, but so it was—for a short time. It was between ten and eleven when the *Wolf* and her prize proceeded on their original course and the sailing ship crossed our course astern. About 1.30 p.m., however, we changed our course and turned about. We were all mystified as to what was going to happen, until we saw a sail on the horizon. The *Wolf's* purpose was evident then. She was going back to destroy the ship whose existence she had forgiven in the morning. Imagine the feelings of the crew of her prey; seeing the *Wolf* bearing down on her in the morning, their suspense as to their fate and that of their ship, their joy at their release, and—here was the *Wolf* again! What would their fate be now? The *Wolf* did not leave them long in doubt. She came up to her prize about 5 p.m. She was a four-masted barque in full sail, in ballast from the Cape to South America, and made a beautiful picture as she lay bathed in floods of golden light from the setting sun. Before dark, however, preparations had begun to remove her officers and crew and provisions, and this was completed in a few hours. We were invited by the Germans to stay up and see the end. They told us a searchlight would be thrown on the ship, that we might better see her go down. Stage effects, with a vengeance! But they were not carried out—it was a too dangerous proceeding, as the enemy regretfully realized. We waited up till past eleven and saw lights flitting about the doomed ship, as the Germans sailors were removing some things, making fast others, and placing the bombs to blow her up. But none waited up for the end, which we heard took place after midnight. The ship first canted over, her sails resting on the water, righted herself and then slowly disappeared. It was a beautiful moonlight night for the commission of so dark a deed. The Germans afterwards told us that when the *Wolf* first spoke the barque she gave her name *Storobrore* and said she was a Norwegian ship, and so was released. The Germans had afterwards discovered from the *Wolf*'s shipping register that she was the *Alec Fawn* and British owned before the war, and therefore to be destroyed.

The Germans told us that on the barque they had seen some English newspapers, and in them was some news of the two men who had escaped from the *Wolf* near Sunday Island. One of them had died while swimming ashore; the other, after some weeks alone on the island, had been picked up by a Japanese cruiser. The news this man was able to give was the first that the outside world had known about the *Wolf* for many months, and the Germans realized that their enemies would be looking out for them and trying to prevent their return to Germany. This man would also be able to give an exact description of the *Wolf*, the names of the ships she had captured before his escape, and the probable fate of other vessels since missing. This, we felt, would bring at least a little comfort to our relatives, who might conclude we were on the raider and not hopelessly lost, as they must have feared.

We had hoped our captors might have put us all on the sailing ship and sent us off on her to South America, as the *Wolf* would have been well away and out of danger before we could have got ashore. But they did not entertain any such idea. Some of us requested that the lifeboats of the sailing ship might be sent over to our ship, as we had only two lifeboats, a couple of small dinghies, and an improvised raft made of barrels and planks lashed together and surrounded by iron uprights and ropes—not sufficient for sixty-five people; but the Germans would not send us these lifeboats, as they said they were leaky!

The question of baggage had to be again reconsidered. It was evident we should be able to save very little, perhaps not even a handbag, if the ship were sunk by the Germans and the prisoners put into the lifeboats. However, we ourselves packed in a handbag our most precious treasures we had brought from Siam. But in case it was impossible to save even so little, we collected the most valuable of our letters and papers and had them sewn up in sailcloth by a German sailor to put in our pockets. The King of Siam had conferred a decoration on me before I left; this was carefully packed and sewn up. I was determined to save this, if nothing else, though it seemed hopeless to expect to save some much-treasured parting presents and addresses presented to me by my Siamese friends. Earlier in my service the King of Siam had conferred another decoration on me, and I was carrying with me His Majesty's Royal Licence for this, signed by him, and also King George V.'s Royal Licence with his Sign-Manual, giving me permission to accept and wear the decoration. Both of these documents, together with others highly valued which I was also determined to save, were secured in water-tight cases, ready to be put in my pockets at the last moment.

On January 8th, when the two ships stopped, the Captain went on to the *Wolf* and brought back with him charts of the North Atlantic and North Sea. We wondered if this would be his farewell visit to and our farewell acquaintance with the *Wolf*, but we remained in company of the *Wolf* for the next few days, and at 7 p.m. on the 10th she again came alongside in the open sea and coaled from us till 4 p.m. on the next day. Conditions were slightly better than on the previous occasion, and the Commander of the *Wolf* was evidently of opinion that they would never again be more favourable, but they were still quite sufficiently unpleasant. More fenders were lost and the *Wolf* was further damaged, and this time our ship also sustained some damage. Some of her plates had been badly dented and she was leaking about a ton and a half an hour. The great uproar caused by the winches going all night, the periodic emptying of ashes dragged in iron buckets over the iron decks, the shifting of coal from the bunkers immediately underneath our cabins, and the constant bumping of the ships made sleep quite out of the question once more, and we were very glad indeed when the *Wolf* sheered off. On this occasion the way in which she came alongside and sheered off was a beautiful piece of seamanship. Not many landsmen, I imagine, have seen this done in absolutely mid-ocean, and not many have been on a ship so lashed alongside another. It was a wonderful experience—would that some friendly hydroplane had seen us from aloft! The two ships lashed together would certainly have presented a strange scene, and could have meant only one thing—a raider and her prize.

On the 11th we again saw and spoke to our *Hitachi* friends on the *Wolf*—the last opportunity we had of speaking to them. They all looked well, but thin. They told us they had been informed that we were going to Spain, and that the *Wolf* with them on board was *not* going to Germany. Some of them believed this, and were comparatively joyful in consequence. But it was only another case of German lies. On the next day we crossed the Equator, and then for some days we saw the *Wolf* no more.

About this time I experienced a little trouble with one of the German sailors. Most of them were courteous and kindly disposed, but one, a boorish, loutish bully, who served us with drinks at table, was a painful exception to this. His name was Fuchs: we sometimes called him Luchs, by mistake, of course! But Fuchs did not think so—he strongly objected to the other name! He had only one eye, and a black shade where the other one should have been. To train his moustache to resemble that of the All-Highest, he wore some apparatus plastered over it, reaching nearly to his eyes and secured behind his ears, so that his appearance was the reverse of prepossessing! I complained to him once about not serving me properly. He waited outside the saloon and cursed me afterwards. "I a German soldier," he said, "not your steward!" I told him that if he had any reason to complain of what I had said or done he should report me to his Captain, and that if he had not done so by six that evening I should report him for insolence. Needless to say, he said nothing to the Captain, so I reported him. The Captain at once thanked me for doing so, called him up at once, and gave him a good wigging. I had no more trouble with him afterwards.

On January 14th I approached the Captain and asked him if the Germans on the *Wolf*, when they got to Germany, would have any means of finding out whether we on the *Igotz Mendi* had safely arrived in Spain. He replied that they would. I then asked him whether, if we were all lost on the *Igotz Mendi* on her return voyage to Spain, the German Government would inform the British Government of our fate. He replied that would certainly be done. I further asked him whether we might send letters to the *Wolf* to have them posted in Germany in the event of our not arriving in Spain. Most of us had to settle up our affairs in some way, in case we might be lost at sea, and wished to write farewell letters to our home people. Some of us, it will be remembered, had already taken some steps in this direction before we were sent on to the *Wolf*, as we thought it possible the *Wolf* might become engaged with a hostile cruiser. We ourselves had to write a farewell letter, among others, to our daughter, born in Siam, from whom we had been separated except for short periods of furlough spent in England, for twelve years. It seemed very hard that after this long separation, and just when we were looking forward to a joyful and fairly speedy reunion, we should perhaps never see her again.

The Captain said we might write these letters, which would not be posted if the *Igotz Mendi* with us on board got back safely to Spain. "But," he added, "we have changed our plans, and now intend that you should be landed in Norway. It will be safer for you all, and you will not have to risk meeting our submarines in the Atlantic again. When we arrive in Norwegian waters the German prize crew will be taken off the ship after the *Wolf* has got home, the ship will be handed over to the Spaniards, and you will all be landed in Norway, from where you can easily make your way to England." Here was quite a new plan—how much truth there was in this declaration will be seen hereafter. From now onwards definite promises began to be made to us concerning the end of our captivity: "In a month you will be free," "The next full moon will be the last you will see at sea," etc., etc.

We were now proceeding north every day, keeping in mid-Atlantic—always well off the trade routes, though of course we crossed some on our way north. The *Wolf*, naturally, was not looking for trouble, and had no intention of putting up a fight if she could avoid it. She was not looking for British warships; what we were anxious to know was whether the British warships were looking for her! On the 19th the Captain again thought he saw distant smoke on the horizon, and we careered about to avoid it as before. But on this occasion we were running away from a cloud! The next day we left the tropics, and with favourable weather were making an average of about 180 knots daily. On several days about this time, we passed through large masses of seaweed drifting from the Sargasso Sea. We did not meet the *Wolf* on the 22nd as our Captain evidently expected to do, and we waited about for her several hours. But next day we did meet her, and we were then told that in eighteen days we should be ashore. We wondered where! We were then about 30° N., and we parted from the *Wolf* the same afternoon. It was always a great relief to us all when we parted from her, keeping our ship's company of prisoners intact. For the men amongst us feared we might all be put upon the *Wolf* to be taken to Germany, leaving our wives on the *Igotz Mendi*. This, so we had been told, had been the intention of the *Wolf's* Commander when the prisoners were first put on the Spanish boat. He had ordered that only women, and prisoners above sixty and under sixteen should be put on the *Igotz Mendi*, but the German doctor, a humane and kindly man, would have nothing to do with this plan and declared he would not be responsible for the health of the women if this were done. So that we owe it to him that wives were not separated from their husbands during this anxious time, as the Commander of the *Wolf* had inhumanly suggested.

Chapter IX – En Route for Ruhleben – Via Iceland

A last effort was made to persuade the Captain to ask the *Wolf*'s Commander to release the Spanish ship here, take all the prize crew off, and send us back to Cape Town (which would have suited the plans of every one of us), for a suspicion began to grow in our minds that Germany, and nowhere else, was the destination intended for us. But our Captain would not listen to this suggestion, and said he was sure the Spanish Captain would not go back to Cape Town even if he promised to do so.

On the next day, January 24th, relief seemed nearer than it had done since our capture four months before. I was sitting on the starboard deck, when suddenly, about 3.30 p.m., I saw coming up out of the mist, close to our starboard bow, what looked like a cruiser with four funnels. The Spanish officer on the bridge had apparently not seen it, or did not want to! Neither, apparently, had the German sailor, if, indeed, he was even on the bridge at that moment. I rushed to inform the American sailing ship Captain of my discovery, and he confirmed my opinion that it was a four-funnelled warship. The Germans were by this time fully alarmed, and the ship slowed down a little; the Captain, evidently also thinking that the vessel was a cruiser, went to his cabin to dispose of the ship's papers, the crew got into their best uniform to surrender, and it looked as if help were at hand at last. We got our precious packages together, put them in our pockets, and got everything ready to leave the ship. We were all out on deck, delighted beyond words (our elation can be imagined), and saw the ship—it must be remembered that it was a very misty day—resolve itself into two two-funnelled ships, apparently transports, one seemingly in distress and very much camouflaged, and the other standing by. Soon, however, they proceeded on their course and crossed our bows fairly close. We were then all ordered to our cabins, and we saw the two ships steam off to the westward, without having spoken us or given any evidence of having seen us at all.

It was a most bitter disappointment to us, comparable to that of shipwrecked sailors on a desert island watching a ship expected to deliver them pass out of sight. Our hopes, raised to such a high pitch, were indeed dashed—we felt very low after this. Would help never come? Better we had not seen the ships than to be deceived and disappointed in this way. But it was a great relief to the Germans. We never discovered what ships they were, but the American said he believed them to be American transports and that each mounted a gun. If only we had seen them the day before, when we were in company with the *Wolf*, they might have been suspicious, and probably have been of some help to us. The Captain was very worried by their appearance, and did not feel that all danger was passed even when the ships disappeared. He feared they might communicate with some armed vessel met with, and give them a description and the position of his ship. Also, had these two ships seen the *Wolf*, from which we had parted only twenty-four hours before?

In the middle of the excitement the Spanish chief mate had rushed on to the bridge into the wireless room, and while the wireless operator was out of the room, or his attention had been diverted, he took from their place all the six or eight bombs on board and threw them overboard. They fell into the sea with a great splash just near where I was standing, but I did not then know it was the bombs which were being got rid of. It was a plucky act, for had he been discovered by the armed sentry while doing it he would have undoubtedly been shot on the spot. On the next day, on the morning of which we saw two sailing ships far distant, an inquiry was held as to the disappearance of the bombs, which would, of course, have been used to sink the ship, and the chief mate owned up. He said that he did it for the sake of the women and children on board; as the sea was rough, their lives would have been in danger if they had been put in the lifeboats when the ship was bombed. He was confined to his cabin for the rest of the voyage, but we managed to see and talk to him from time to time, and thanked him for his bravery. Later he was sentenced by the Commander of the *Wolf* to three years' imprisonment in Germany and a fine of 2,000 marks. From this time all the Spanish officers were relieved of their duties.

The Germans had told us that, in the event of the prize being captured while the weather was rough, the ship would not be bombed or sunk, as they had no desire to endanger the lives of the women or children amongst us. In fact, so they said, the ship would not be bombed under any conditions when once the *Wolf* had got all the coal she wanted. It was indeed difficult to see what purpose would be served by the Germans sinking the Spanish ship, if she were overhauled by an Allied cruiser. The Allies could not keep her, as she would have to be restored to Spain; the Germans said they would not keep her, but return her to her owners. To have deliberately sunk her would only have meant a gratuitous offence to Spain. Nevertheless, the next time we met the *Wolf* a new supply of bombs and hand grenades was put on board our ship. At the same time an extra Lieutenant came on board, additional neutrals were sent over to help work the ship, and the prize crew was increased from nine to nineteen. All the prize crew now wore caps with the words "S.M.S. *Otter*" inscribed thereon. Somewhere about this time the American Captain and the second mate of one of the captured ships had returned to them their instruments which had been taken from them at the time of their capture.

The Kaiser's birthday, which fell on a Sunday, was honoured by the sacrifice of the last calf, and was marked by a most terrific storm. The wind was raging for hours at a hurricane force between eleven and twelve, the seas were between thirty and forty feet high, and it seemed impossible that the ship could live in such a sea. It seemed that she must inevitably founder. But notwithstanding terrible rolling, she shipped very little water, but all of the prisoners were alarmed at the rough weather and the rolling of the ship. The wireless aerials were brought down by the storm, and any seas that did come on board smashed whatever deck hamper had been left about.

From this day onwards we lived in a condition of great misery, and death stared us in the face many times. The prospect was a gloomy one: just when my wife and I had reached the time to which we had been looking forward for many years it seemed daily increasingly unlikely that our lives could escape a violent and brutal ending. Such thoughts inevitably occurred to our minds during these dark and anxious days. But there was still to come even worse than we had yet experienced. It got colder and colder every day for a considerable time; the food got worse and worse, and we were on short rations; the ship became more and more dirty, smokes ran short—only some ancient dusty shag brought from Germany by the *Wolf* and some virulent native tobacco from New Guinea remained—and conditions generally became almost beyond endurance. Darkness fell very early in these far northern latitudes, and the long nights were very dreary and miserable. What wretched nights we spent in that crowded saloon—crushed round the table attempting to read or play cards! It was too dismal and uncomfortable for words, but we had either to endure that or our cold, wet cabins. Sundays seemed to be the days on which the worst storms occurred, though on very few of the days from this time onwards did we have anything but very dirty weather. The Australian stewardess became very ill with asthma, and with no adequate medicine supply on board, no suitable food, and no warm or dry cabin for her, it is indeed a miracle that she lived through these last few weeks. She owes her life to the devotion of the Australian Major of the A.M.C. on board and the lady prisoners who assisted in nursing her.

On February 5th we again met the *Wolf*—we had sighted her on the evening of the 4th, but it was too rough then to communicate, and, it was said, the *Wolf* did not recognize our rocket signals. With the *Wolf*'s usual luck, the weather moderated next day, and the ships stopped. Just as the Germans on land always seemed to get the weather they wanted, so they were equally favoured at sea. This was noticed over and over again, and the *Hitachi* passengers had very good reason to be sick about this. The two days previous to her capture the sea had been so rough that the "bird" could not go up, but on the actual day of the capture the sea had very much calmed down, enabling the seaplane to go up and spot the *Hitachi's* position.

Those who had written letters to be sent on the *Wolf* sent them over on this day, and the Spanish chief mate expected to be sent on the *Wolf*, as we might not meet her again. Luckily for him, however, for some reason or other he was not transferred that day, and neither he nor we ever saw the *Wolf* again after the morning of February 6th. Doubtless the *Wolf* expected to meet us again before the final separation occurred, when the transference of the officer would have been effected.

We heard from the *Wolf* that she was getting very short of food, and that there was much sickness, including many cases of scurvy, on board. The pigeons must have gone the way of all flesh by this time, and perhaps the dachshunds had too—in the form of German sausages! Some of the prisoners, we knew, had very little clothing, and positively none for cold weather, and our hearts were sore at the thought of so many of our fellow-countrymen, many of whom we had known, in good and ill fortune, being taken into captivity in Germany.

The next day we entered the Arctic Circle. The cold was intense, the cabins were icy, the temperature falling as low as 14° F. in some of them. There was no heating apparatus on the ship, with the exception of a couple of small heating pipes in the saloon. These were usually covered with the officers' thick clothes, and some of the passengers' garments drying. The cabin curtains froze to the ports; all the cabin roofs leaked, and it was impossible to keep the floors and bedding dry; and in our cabin, in addition, we had water constantly flowing and swishing backwards and forwards between the iron deck of the ship and the wooden floor of the cabin. This oozed up through the floor and accumulated under the settee, and on many nights we emptied five or six buckets full of icy water from under the settee, which had also to be used as a bed. At last I persuaded the Captain to allow one of the sailors to drill a hole in the side of the cabin so that the water could have an outlet on to the deck. I had asked that this might be done directly the water appeared in our cabin, but was told it was *against the regulations of the Board of Trade*! Quoting the Board of Trade under such conditions—was this a sample of German humour? We managed to secure a piece of matting for our cabin floor—it was soaked through every day, but we had it dried daily in the engine-room. Since the great storm on the Kaiser's birthday our feet had never been dry or warm, and were in this condition till some hours after we got ashore.

The ports of the cabins had all long ago been painted black in order that no light might show through, and the darkness at night, especially in these stormy seas, was always very sinister and ugly, not to say dangerous—not a spark of light showing on deck. We had to sit in these cold and dark cabins during the day. The weather prevented us from being on deck, which was often covered with frost and snow, and often there was nowhere else to sit. The electric light was on for only a limited time each day, so, as the ports could not be opened, it being far too cold, we asked and obtained permission to scratch a little of the paint off the ports in our cabin. This made things a little more bearable, but it can easily be imagined how people who had been living in tropical climates for many years fared under such conditions. As for our own case, my wife had spent only two winters out of Siam during the last twenty years, while I had spent none during the last twenty-one, and it is no exaggeration to say that we suffered agonies with the cold. It was nothing short of cruel to expose women and children to this after they had been dragged in captivity over the seas for many months. The Captain had ordered a part of the bunkers to be cleared, so that the prisoners might sit there in the cold weather. But the place was so dirty and uncomfortable, and difficult of access, in addition to it being in darkness, and quite unprovided with seats, that most of the prisoners preferred the crowded little saloon. Luchs was provided with a swanky kennel for the cold weather. The Spanish carpenter contrived it, and it looked like a small model of a Norwegian church—painted the Allied grey! Even the Captain's dog was more comfortable than we were!

On the morning of February 7th we for the first time encountered icefloes, when attempting the northern passage between Greenland and Iceland. About 11 a.m. we stopped and hooted for the *Wolf*, as a fog had come on—the first time we had heard a steamer's siren since the day of our capture. We waited for some hours in the ice, but no answering signal came, so the Captain decided to turn back, as he thought it impossible to force his way through the ice. We therefore went back again on our course, the

Captain hoping that the wind would change and cease blowing the icefloes from off the shores of Greenland.

That morning is unforgettable. The cold fog, the great bergs of ice floating by the ship and sometimes crashing into her, the dreary sea, the cold, filthy, miserable ship, our hopeless condition, all helped to lower our spirits, and we felt we had plumbed the very depths of misery.

After a day or two slow steaming on this course and occasional stopping altogether—what dreary, miserable, hopeless days!—we resumed our attempt to go to the north of Iceland, evidently to escape the attention of the British ships which the Germans expected to encounter between the south of Iceland and the Faroes. But before long it became evident that ice was still about, and in the darkness of the early morning of February 11th we bumped heavily against icebergs several times. This threw some of us out of our bunks; once again there was no more sleep during the night. This time the Captain abandoned his attempt to go through the northern passage, and turned the ship round to try his luck in the passage he did not expect to be so free from British attentions.

We thought perhaps that as we were on short rations and even drinking water was running short, and the case of us all really desperate, the Captain would land us and give up the ship at Reykjavik, leaving us there to be rescued. Even a stay in Iceland would be better than one in Germany, for which country we now all suspected we were bound. The uncertainty concerning our ultimate destination added to our miseries, and these were not lessened when on February 11th the Captain told us, *for the first time* that it was, and always had been, the intention to take us on the *Igotz Mendi* to Germany, there to be interned in civilian prisoners' camps. He told us, too, that the women and those of the men over military age would be released at once, but we all declined to believe anything else our captors told us, as they had deliberately and repeatedly deceived us by assuring us at various times they were going to land us in Spain, or Norway, or some other neutral country. The string of German lies must surely by now be ended. But no! There were still more to come, as will be seen later on.

At daylight on the 11th we were still among icefloes, but going away from instead of meeting them, and on that morning we saw in the distance the coast of Iceland, which the Germans tried to persuade us was the sails of fishing boats, as they did not wish us to think we were so near the Icelandic coast, the first land that we had seen since the Maldive Islands, a week after our capture, i.e. more than four months before. We also saw a few fishing boats off the coast.

We now shaped a course for the coast of Norway, keeping to the north of the Faroes. On Sunday, the 17th, we again ran into a very heavy storm. Ever since the storm on January 27th the propeller had been constantly racing and sending shudders through the ship from stem to stern. On this day this feature, which was always disconcerting and to a certain extent alarming, became more marked, and the thud with which the ship met the seas more and more loud, so loud indeed that on one occasion the Captain thought we had struck a mine, and rushed from the saloon to the bridge to ascertain what damage had been done. Luckily for us, the engines were British made. No inferior workmanship could possibly have stood the terrific strain put on these engines during these weeks of terrible storms. The Captain and crew had by this time become very anxious as to the fate of the *Wolf*, as no news had been received concerning her. Day after day the Captain told us he expected news, but they went by without any being received. But on the evening of the 19th the Captain informed us that he had received a wireless message announcing the safe arrival of the *Wolf* at a German port. The Germans seemed singularly little elated at the news, and hardly ever mentioned the subject again after that evening. This was so different from what we had expected that most of the prisoners did not believe the *Wolf* had got home. We hoped that she had been intercepted and captured by a British cruiser, and that with any luck a similar fate might be in store for us.

The *Wolf* had certainly made a wonderful cruise, and the Germans were naturally very proud of it—almost the only exploit of their navy of which they reasonably could be proud. They had successfully evaded the enemy for fifteen months, and had kept their ship in good repair, for they had first-class mechanics and engineers on board. But she must have been very weather-worn and partly crippled before she arrived at a home port. She had touched at no port or no shore from the day she left Germany till the day she returned to the Fatherland. She was, too, the only German raider which had extended her operations beyond the Atlantic. The *Wolf* had cruised and raided in the Indian and Pacific Oceans as well. She had sunk seven steamers and seven sailing ships, and claimed many more ships sunk as a result of her mine-laying. Besides the prizes already named, she had captured and sunk the *Turritella*, *Wordsworth*, *Jumna*, *Dee*, *Winslow*, and *Encore*, the last three of which were sailing vessels. Her first prize, the *Turritella*, taken in February 1917 in the Indian Ocean, was originally a German ship, a sister of the *Wolf*, captured by the British. On her recapture by the Germans, she was equipped as a raider and mine-layer, and sent off on an expedition by herself. But soon afterwards near Aden she encountered a British warship, when the prize crew scuttled her and surrendered.

Chapter X. Saved by Shipwreck

The Germans were now getting very anxious as they approached the blockade zone. They affected, however, to believe that there was no blockade, and that there was no need of one now that America was in the war. "No one will trade with us," they said; "accordingly there is no need of a blockade." But, as some of the passengers remarked to the Captain, "If there is no blockade, as the Germans say, why haven't you more raiders out, instead of only one, and why have so few been able to come out?" There was, of course, no answer to this! The Captain further remarked that even if there were a blockade it would always be possible to get through it at the week-end, as all the British blockading fleet returned to port for that time! The *Wolf*, he said, came out and got home through the blockade at the week-end. It was quite simple; we were to do the same, and we should be escorted by submarines, as the *Wolf* had been on both occasions.

Nevertheless, the Germans were at great pains to keep as far as possible from any place in which British ships might appear. But unfortunately not one did appear, here or anywhere else, to rescue us, although we felt certain in our own minds that some of our ships would be present and save us in these parts of the seas, which we believed were regularly patrolled. What meetings, discussions, and consultations we had in our wretched tiny cabin during these dreadful days and nights! We had cheered ourselves up for a long time past that the *Wolf* would never get through the British blockade, and that some friendly vessel would surely be the means of our salvation. The Spanish officers who had had experience of the blockade also assured us that no vessel could possibly get through unchallenged; and we, in our turn, had assured the American captives among us of the same thing. There was no fog to help the enemy, the condition of the moon was favourable to us, and we had pointed out to each other on maps various places where there *must* be British ships on the watch. It was a bitter disappointment to us that we saw none. It was heartbreaking. We had built so much on our hopes; it was galling beyond words for the enemy to be in the right and ourselves mistaken. But, after all, we reflected, what is one ship in this vast expanse of stormy seas? In vain we tried to derive some comfort from this. But, alas! *we* were on that one ship, which fact made all the difference! We had been "hanging our hats" on the British Navy for so long—surely we were not mistaken! Surely, to change the metaphor, we were not going to be let down after all! The British Navy, we knew, never let anybody down; but in our condition of protracted physical and nervous depression, it was not to be wondered at that thoughts of hopelessness were often present in our minds.

The "Igotz Mendi" ashore at Skagen. Taken on the morning of our rescue.

On the 20th we were off Bergen, and saw the coast in the distance. I suggested to the Captain that it would save much trouble if he would land us there. He replied that he would very much like to, but was afraid it was quite impossible! I further asked him whether, if we were ultimately rescued, he would give us a pass conferring further immunity from capture at sea by the enemy, as we felt we had had more than our share of captivity at sea. He said he was afraid that would be against regulations! The next day we were nearer the coast and saw a couple of suspicious steam trawlers which gave the Germans a few anxious moments, and on that night we encountered the greatest storm we experienced on the cruise. The wind was terrific, huge seas broke over the ship, the alley-way outside the cabins was awash all the night, and the water even invaded the saloon to a small extent. Articles and receptacles for water that had not been made absolutely fast in the cabins were tossed about; many cabins were drenched and running with water. The noise of the wind howling and the seas breaking on the deck was so alarming to those in the outside cabins that they left the cabins, waded up the alley-way, and assembled in the saloon, though sleep that night was utterly impossible there or anywhere else on the ship. The German officers when coming off watch came to the saloon and assured us that things were all right and that there was no danger, but the Spanish Captain was very concerned as to the treatment his ship was receiving both at the hands of the elements and those of the Germans, who frankly said they cared nothing about the condition of the ship provided they got her into Germany. The ship, though steaming full speed, made no progress that night, but went back, and in three days, the 19th, 20th, and 21st, made only 100 knots.

After such stormy nights, and in such bitter cold weather, a breakfast of cold canned crab, or dry bread with sugar, or rice and hot water plus a very little gravy, or bread and much watered condensed milk, was not very nourishing or satisfying, but very often that was all we had. The food we had was just sufficient to keep us alive, and that was all. This weather of course pleased the German Captain, who said that no enemy ship would or could board him under such conditions. In fact, he said no enemy vessel would be out of port in such weather! Only those supermariners, the Germans, could manage a ship under similar conditions! He told us we were much safer on the *Igotz Mendi* than we should be on a British cruiser, which might at any time be attacked by a German armed ship. "I would rather die on a British cruiser to-night," my wife retorted, "than be a prisoner in Germany," an opinion we all endorsed. The weather alone was sufficiently terrifying to the landsmen amongst us; the prospect of having to take to the lifeboats at any moment if the Germans took it in into their heads to sink the ship if she were sighted by an enemy ship added to the fears of all of us. None of us dared undress thoroughly before turning in—when we did turn in, lifebelts were always kept handy, and we had to be ready for any emergency at any moment. And, as will be readily understood, our imaginations had been working horribly during the last few months, especially since we began to encounter the rough weather and the winter gales in the grey and cheerless wastes of the North Atlantic. The natural conditions were bad enough in all conscience. But, in addition, we had the knowledge that if we survived them we were going into German captivity. Could anything be worse?

There had been no boat drill, and the lifeboat accommodation was hopelessly inadequate for more than eighty people now on board. It is certain, with the mixed crew on board, that there would have been a savage fight for the boats. The prospect, looked at from any point of view, was alarming, and one of the greatest anxiety for us all. Physical distress and discomfort were not the only things we had to contend with—the nervous strain was also very great, and seemed endless.

On February 22nd we rounded the Naze. Here, we thought, we should certainly come across some British vessel. But that day and the next passed—it seemed as if we too were to get in during the week-end!—and hope of rescue disappeared. Many messages had been dropped overboard in bottles and attached to spars, etc., during the voyage, but all, apparently, in vain. The bearing of the Germans towards us became markedly changed, discipline more rigid, and still greater care was taken that no vestige of light showed anywhere at night. We were almost in their clutches now, the arrival at Kiel and transference to Ruhleben were openly talked of, and our captors showed decided inclination to jeer at us and our misfortunes. We were told that all diaries, if we had kept them, must be destroyed, or we should be severely punished when we arrived in Germany. Accordingly, those of us who had kept diaries made ready to destroy them, but fortunately did not do so. I cut the incriminating leaves out of mine, ready to be torn up and thrown overboard. I had written my diary in Siamese characters during the whole time, so the Germans could not have gained much information from it.

Sunday, February 24th, dawned, a cold, cheerless day. "I

suppose this time next week we shall be going to church in Kiel," said one of the prisoners to the chief mate at breakfast. "Or," the latter replied, "I might be going to church with my brother, who is already a prisoner in the Isle of Man!" We were now in the comparatively narrow waters of the Skager-Rack, and we saw only one vessel here, a Dutch fishing boat. Our last chance had nearly gone. Most of us were now resigned to our fate and saw no hope—in fact, I had written in my diary the day before, "There is no hope left, no boat of ours to save us"—but some said we still might see a British war vessel when we rounded the Skaw. At mid-day the sailor on the look-out came into the saloon and reported to the Captain that a fog was coming on. "Just the weather I want," he exclaimed, rubbing his hands. "With this lovely fog we shall round the Skaw and get into German waters unobserved." It looked, indeed, as if our arrival in Germany were now a dead certainty.

But the fog that the Captain welcomed was just a little too much for him; it was to prove his undoing rather than his salvation. The "Good old German God," about whom we had heard so much, was not going to see them through this time. For once, *we* were to be favoured. The white fog thickened after the mid-day meal, and, luckily for us, it was impossible to see far ahead. Soon after two we passed a floating mine, and we knew that before long we should be going through a minefield—not a very cheerful prospect with floating mines round us in a fog, especially as the Captain admitted that the position of the mines might have been altered since he last had knowledge of their exact situation! But we were all too far gone to care now; and some of us gathered together in our cold and gloomy cabin were discussing the prospects and conditions of imprisonment in Germany and attempting to console ourselves with the reflection that even internment at Ruhleben could not be worse than the captivity we had experienced on the high seas, when, at 3.30 on that Sunday afternoon, we felt a slight bump, as if the ship had touched bottom. Then another bump, and then still one more! We were fast! Were we really to be saved at the very last minute? It began to look like it, like the beginning of the end, but it would not do to build too much on this slender foundation. The engines continued working, but no progress was made; they were reversed—still no movement.

One of the men amongst us was so overjoyed that he attempted a very premature somersault in the saloon. He was sure it was to be a case of "Hooray for our side" this time! What thoughts of freedom, what hopes flashed through our minds! The fog was fairly thick, but we could just make out through it the line of the shore and the waves breaking on it some distance away, and two sirens were going at full blast, one from a lightship and one from a lighthouse. The Captain, luckily from our point of view, had mistaken one for the other, and so had run aground. The German officers became agitated; with great difficulty a boat was got out—what chance should we have had if we had had to leave the ship in haste at any time?—soundings made, and various means adopted to work the ship off, but all were of no avail. The Captain admitted that his charts of this particular spot were not new and not good. Again how lucky for us! It was impossible to tell the state of the tide at this moment; we all hoped it might be high tide, for then our rescue would be certain. The engines were set to work from time to time, but no movement could be made. Darkness fell, and found us still stuck fast. Our spirits had begun to rise, the prospect was distinctly brighter, and soon after six o'clock the Assistant Lieutenant went ashore in mufti to telephone to the nearest port, Frederikshavn, for help. What reply he received we never heard, but we *did* hear that he reported he was on a German ship from Bergen to Kiel and wanted help. Lourenço Marques to Kiel, via Iceland, would have been nearer the truth!

About eight o'clock we heard from one of the neutrals among the crew that the Captain of a salvage tug was shortly coming aboard to inquire into matters. The ladies among us decided to stay in the saloon while the Captain of the tug interviewed the German Captain in the chartroom above it. On the arrival of the tug Captain on the bridge, the ladies in the saloon created a veritable pandemonium, singing, shrieking, and laughing at the top of their voices. It sounded more like a Christmas party than one of desperate prisoners in distress. The Danish

Captain departed; what had been the result of his visit we did not know, but at any rate he knew there were women on board. The German Captain came down into the saloon, asked pleasantly enough what all the noise was about, and said, "I have offered the salvage people £5,000 to tow the ship off; money is nothing to us Germans. This will be done at four to-morrow morning, and we shall then proceed on our way to Kiel."

Some of us had talked over a plan suggested by the second mate of a captured ship, by which one of the neutrals among the crew should contrive to go ashore in one of the tug's boats in the darkness, communicate with the nearest British Consul, and inform him of the situation and the desperate case we were in. We promised him £500, to be raised among the "saloon passengers," if by so doing our rescue should be accomplished.

We remained in the saloon talking over developments when we heard that a Danish gunboat had come nearly alongside, and that her Commander was coming on board. He had presumably received a report from the Captain of the tug. We heard afterwards that he had his suspicions about the ship, and had brought with him on board one of his own men to make inquiries of the crew, among whom were Norwegians, Swedes, and Danes, while he kept the German Commander busy in the saloon. The previous mistake of taking the Danish Captain on to the bridge was not to be repeated. The Commander of the gunboat was to come into the saloon. So the ladies could not remain there and make their presence known. But some of them contrived to leave some of their garments on the table and settee in the saloon—a muff, hats, gloves, etc. These the Danish Commander must have seen; and not only that, for he saw some ladies who had stood in one door of the saloon before they were sent to their cabins, when he entered at the other one. He also saw the Australian Major of the A.M.C., in khaki, and other passengers standing with the ladies in the alley-way. If he had entertained any suspicions as to the correct character of the ship, which the Germans were of course trying to conceal, they must have been strongly confirmed by now. It was now too late for us to be sent to our cabins, as a German sailor came and ordered. We had achieved our object.

It was a night of great unrest, but finally most of us lay down in our clothes. For very many nights we had been unable to rest properly owing to the violence of the weather, the possibility of having to leave the ship at any moment, and our general anxiety concerning our desperate condition. We had not had our clothes off for many days. At 4 a.m. we heard the engines working, as the Captain had told us they would, but still no movement of the ship could be felt. How we prayed that the ship might refuse to budge! She *did* refuse, and soon the engines ceased working; it was evident then that the attempt to get the ship off must for the present be given up. The wind was rising and the sea getting rougher, and at 6 a.m. a German sailor came and knocked at the doors of all the cabins, saying, "Get up, and pack your baggage and go ashore." *We were to go ashore? We, who had not seen the shore for months, and had never expected to land on any, much less a free one, were to go ashore?* Were we dreaming? No, it was true, though it seemed too good to be believed. Never was order more willingly and gladly obeyed! But first we had to see how the ship stood with regard to the shore; we went out on deck to look—there was the blessed green shore less than half a mile away, the first really solid earth we had seen close at hand since we left Colombo exactly five months before. Only those who have seen nothing but the sea for many months can imagine with what a thrill of joy we saw the shore and realized that we were saved at last. We had seen the sea under nearly every aspect possible, from the Equator to the Arctic regions, and we had appreciated more than ever before its vastness. And yet in all these months, travelling these thousands of miles, we had, besides the few vessels already mentioned, seen hardly any ships! We had been under shell-fire, taken prisoner, had lived on board a German raider and in her evil company many months, had been in lifeboats once in the open sea, were about to go in once more, in a rough sea, to be rescued from captivity, had seen our ship sunk and another one captured and scuttled, had been through terrific wintry weather in the North Atlantic, among icebergs, in the submarine zone, and on the very borders of an enemy minefield!—experiences that perhaps no other landsmen have passed through! Not many of us wish for sea travel again.

Lieutenant Rose came along and told us to hurry, or we might not be able to get off, as the sea was getting rougher every minute. We *did* hurry indeed, and it did not take us long to dress and throw our things into our bags. When we had done so and were ready to go to the lifeboats, we were told that we might take no baggage whatever, as the lifeboat was from a shore station and could save lives only, not baggage.

The German Captain took his bad luck in good part, but he was, of course, as sick as we were rejoiced at the turn events had taken. He had known the night before he could get no help from the Danish authorities, as they refused towing assistance till all the passengers had been taken off the ship. But he had hoped to get off unaided at four in the morning, and he was not going to admit defeat and loss till they were absolutely certain. He professed great anger with the Danes, saying that if they had only helped as he requested, the ship could have been towed off in the night, and we with all our baggage could have been landed at a Danish port alongside a pier the next morning, instead of having to leave all our baggage behind on the ship. I fancy not many of us believed this; if the ship had been got off we should have brought up at Kiel, and not at any Danish port. And, as the tug Captain said afterwards, if he had towed the ship off the Germans would have most likely cut the hawser directly afterwards, he would have received no pay for his work, and we certainly should not have landed in Denmark.

It was a terrible blow for Lieutenant Rose; enough to put an end to his prospects in the Imperial German Navy. Let us pay a tribute to a fallen enemy, for such he now became. It is pleasing to be able to record, in a German-made war which has crowded into its four years such heartbreaking sorrow, misery, horror, and destruction as has surely never been known in a similar period in the world's history, and with Germany's unparalleled record of wickedness and calculated cruelty to her captives and those she wished to terrorize on land and sea, that there were still remaining *some* Germans who had retained some idea of more humane treatment towards those who had the misfortune to fall into their hands. Fortunately for us, Lieutenant Rose was one of these—a striking contrast to the devils in his country's U boats. He had succeeded in maintaining not unfriendly relations with his captives, and had on the whole done his best for them under the conditions prevailing. He had evaded capture for fifteen months, and had skilfully carried his ship through terrible storms and many other perils—*almost* to port. Now, just at the very last moment when it seemed absolutely certain he would get his prize home and reap his reward, his hopes were dashed, and failure, blank and utter failure, was the result. But the death of his hopes meant for us the resurrection of ours, and his failure, freedom for us all.

Chapter XI. Free at Last

A fine lifeboat, manned by sturdy Danish sailors, was alongside the ship; the sea was very rough, but our ship steady, firmly embedded in the sandy bottom, and driven farther in since she stranded. The packages we had decided to save at any cost were put in our pockets, lifebelts and life-saving waistcoats once more put on, and once more we all climbed a ship's ladder, but as the lifeboat was rising and falling almost the height of the ship with the heavy seas, descent into it was not easy. One by one we dropped into the outstretched arms of the sailors as the boat rose on the crest of a wave to the bottom of the ladder. It was a trying moment, but nothing mattered now; once over the side of the ship, we were no longer in German hands, and were *free*! The waves dashed over and drenched us as we sat in the lifeboat; we were sitting in icy water, all of us more or less wet through. At last the lifeboat crew pulled for the shore, the high seas sweeping over us all the way. We grounded on the beach, the sturdy sailors carried some, others jumped into the water and waded ashore, and we were all on terra firma, free at last, after weary months of waiting and captivity. Groups of villagers were waiting on the beach to welcome us even at this early hour. They plied us with questions as far as they could, and great was their wonder at what we had to tell.

The Skagen lifeboat going out to the "Igotz Mendi" to bring off the prisoners.

The Skagen lifeboat bringing tosShore the prisoners from the „Igotz Mendi".

We had been saved at the eleventh hour, almost the fifty-ninth minute of it; we were almost in German waters, at the very gates of Germany, being due at Kiel the very next day. It was a miraculous escape if ever there was one, and came at a moment when all hope had gone. Would that the *Wolf* had gone ashore in the same place! All our fellow-countrymen on board her would then have been free, and they could have given information and saved us as well.

What emotions surged within us as we trod the free earth once more! What we had gone through since we were last on shore! Then it was on British soil; now it was on that of a friendly neutral country. It seemed strange to be treading land again after five months on shipboard. How welcome to see the green fields, the horses at work on the beach, the people in the village, the village itself! How good it all was! We had escaped imprisonment with the enemy, escaped making acquaintance with the notorious Ruhleben of evil fame. The more we reflected on it — and we did so every minute — the more wonderful did our escape appear. But our thoughts also turned to our friends on the *Wolf* who were doomed to meet the cruel fate from which we had so mercifully been delivered.

Once on dry land, and escorted by the villagers, we walked over the sandhills to the lighthouse, about half a mile away. There we were received with open arms. The kindly Danes could not do enough for us. We had only what we stood up in; we dried our clothes, other dry garments were offered us, hot drinks and food were supplied liberally, and we were generally made much of. We had come back to life and warmth once more. The lighthouse staff and villagers vied with each other in their efforts to make us feel at home and comfortable. Some of the sailors and fishermen even offered us part of their own breakfasts and dinners, which were wrapped up in handkerchiefs, ready to take to their work. The bonny rosy-cheeked Danish girls aired all the English they knew, and wanted to hear all about it; the jolly children danced round with joy when they heard the wonderful story of our deliverance. Every one, from the charming and dignified head of police who heard our story and examined our passports, to the humblest village child, rejoiced at our escape. The good motherly folk at the lighthouse fairly bubbled over with joy as they chattered and poured out sympathy and busied themselves with attending to our creature comforts.

After interviews with some Danish Government officials we were taken to hotels in Skagen, the nearest town, a small summer bathing resort, just to the south of the Skaw. It was a gloriously clear, bright, and sunny day, though very windy and cold, and the condition of the fields showed that "February fill dyke" had been living up to its reputation. Some of us walked into Skagen, and on the way heard the most enchanting sounds we had heard for months—the songs of skylarks—music which we certainly had never expected to hear again. Our spirits were as bright as the larks' on that day, and the birds seemed to be putting into music for us the joy and gratitude we felt in our hearts. The ladies were, of course, too exhausted to walk, and my wife got a lift in a cart in which a Danish girl and a man were proceeding to Skagen. They asked her endless questions, and she expressed her opinions very strongly on the German treatment of their prisoners, and of the endless lies they had told us. On arrival at Skagen we discovered that the man was the German Consul at that town! So, for once in his life, he heard the truth about his countrymen!

After lunch, the first square meal we had had for months, we set off to telegraph to our relatives and friends, to announce we were still in the world. It was one of our greatest anxieties on board that we could not communicate with our friends, who we knew would be grieving over our disappearance and, we feared, would have given us up for lost, for we had been out of communication with the outside world for five months. Never daring to hope that an opportunity to despatch it might ever occur, I had many a time mentally framed a cablegram which, in the fewest possible words, should tell our friends of our adventures since we disappeared from human ken. But the long-delayed opportunity had at last arrived, and our wildest hopes and dreams were realized. They had become solid fact, and the words flashed over the wires from Denmark to friends in Siam and relatives in England were: "Captured September 26th—proceeding Germany—ashore

Denmark—lifeboat rescue—both well." The last two words were not, of course, strictly true, but they would at least serve to reassure our friends that we had been less unfortunate than only too many British captives in German hands.

The same afternoon we walked back to the beach to see if we could go aboard the stranded ship to retrieve our luggage, but the sea was far too rough to allow of this, and the German and Spanish crew had not been taken off. While on the beach we saw two floating mines exploded by a Danish gunboat. We had not only had a narrow escape from the Germans, but also from the dangers of a minefield. The next day was also too rough for us to go aboard; in fact, it was so rough that the lifeboat went out and took everybody off the ship, both Spanish and German. The Spanish first mate was thus saved, and after all did not serve his sentence in Germany. We congratulated him once more on his lucky escape. He had escaped even more than we had. It was reported that a German submarine appeared to take off the German officers on this day, but as it was too rough to lower the boats this could not be contrived.

The *Igotz Mendi* was now deserted, but as the Danish authorities had adjudged her, twenty-four hours after her stranding, to be a Spanish ship, she had reverted to her original owners. Accordingly, before leaving her the Spanish Captain had hoisted the Spanish flag at her stern, the first time that or any other flag had appeared there since that November morning when the Germans had captured her far away in the Indian Ocean. She was no longer a German prize. She would have been the only one the *Wolf* had secured to take home—a neutral ship with only a few tons of coal on board, and a few married couples, and sick and elderly men as prisoners—not much to show for a fifteen months' cruise; and even that small prey was denied the Germans, though the *Wolf* had certainly carried home a valuable cargo and some hundreds of prisoners, besides doing considerable damage to the shipping of the Allies.

The position of the stranded ship was a unique one. She was a neutral ship, a German prize, stranded in neutral waters, with a crew composed of Germans and neutral prisoners, and carrying twenty passenger prisoners of many enemy nationalities—English, Australian, American, Japanese, Chinese, and Indian; of these fifteen were European, and in the company were nine women and two children.

Never was there a more dramatic turning of the tables; the Germans were now interned and we were free. The German officers were sent off under guard to an inland town, and the sailors sent to a camp in another part of Denmark. The sailors did not attempt to disguise their joy at the turn events had taken. On their return to Germany they would have had a few weeks' leave and then done duty in a submarine or at the front. Now, they were interned in a land where there was at least much more to eat than they could have hoped for in Germany, and their dangers were at an end till the war was over. They were marched under an armed guard of Danes up and down the village street several times on one of these days; they were all smiles, singing as they marched along.

The next day a hurricane was still blowing, and going aboard was still out of the question. The ship was blown farther in shore, and it began to look as if she would break up and we should see nothing of our personal belongings. The day after, however, was beautifully fine, and we left Skagen harbour in two motor barges, almost touching a floating mine on the way. It took more than an hour to get from the harbour to the ship, for we had to take a very circuitous route owing to the shallow water and many sandbanks. It was a bitterly cold trip, but at last we reached and with great difficulty—as no gangway was down and we had to climb a ladder projecting a few feet out from the ship's side—boarded the ship, which was in charge of the Danish authorities. After some difficulty, for the ship was in a state of great chaos, we secured from various parts of the ship all our baggage, which was landed that night at Skagen, much to our relief, as up to that time we had only what we stood up in at the time we landed from the lifeboat. So that, after all, we lost very little of our baggage, a most unexpected stroke of good luck. Some of us returned to the shore, only a short distance away, in the salvage tug's lifeboat, as we did not relish the long return trip in the motor barges, crammed as they would be with baggage. From there we walked to our hotel. The baggage was taken to the Custom House, and next day put on the train, so we were unable to open it till we arrived in Copenhagen, by which time we stood badly in need of it.

We had set foot on the *Igotz Mendi* for the last time. She had been our "home" for more than three months—never shall we forget her. I can picture every detail of her as I write, the tiny cabins, the miserable tiled floor saloon, and the wretched meals taken therein, the dirty condition of the whole ship, the iron decks—none of it will ever be forgotten by any one of her unwilling passengers.

The *Igotz Mendi* was some time afterwards towed off into deep water, and after repairs left Danish waters and proceeded to Spain, after loading up with a full cargo of coal at Newcastle. Wonderful to relate—for it is indeed a marvel that the Germans did not make a special and successful effort to sink her—she arrived at her home port, Bilbao, on June 21, 1918, with her whole ship's company complete. She had naturally a great reception, being welcomed with flags, bands, and fireworks. What an adventurous voyage she had had since she last left European waters! We owe a great deal to her genial Captain and all her officers and crew, who one and all did what they could for us and were invariably kind and sympathized with us in our misfortunes and rejoiced with us at our escape. It may even have been due to the gentle persuasion of her Spanish crew that the *Igotz Mendi* made such a thorough job of running aground at Skagen. The Spaniards naturally regarded their captors with no friendly eye, and were as anxious as we were that their ship should not get to Germany.

During the week we had to give evidence to the Danish authorities concerning our capture and treatment on board. We were overwhelmed with kindness by the Danes, who made no secret of their sympathies with the Allies; invitations to dinners and parties flowed in, and we could not have accepted them all if we had stayed as many weeks as we had days.

On Friday, March 1st, at 1 p.m., most of us left Skagen. The whole village turned out to give us a good send-off, and snapshots galore were taken—this, indeed, had been going on ever since we landed. The ladies among us were presented with flowers and chocolates, the men with smokes, and we left with the heartiest good wishes of our warm-hearted hosts. While in Denmark we read the German account of the *Wolf's* expedition and exploits. It was, of course, grossly exaggerated, and contained a fantastic account of the "action" between the *Wolf* and *Hitachi*. Rather a one-sided "action," as the *Wolf* did all the firing!

From Skagen our passage home was arranged by the British Consular authorities. The journey from Skagen to Copenhagen was rather trying, since we had to leave the too well-heated train during the night and embark on train ferries when crossing from mainland to island and from one island to another. It was bitterly cold. We made our first acquaintance with bread and butter tickets at Skagen, and found them also in use on the railways and train ferries in Denmark and Scandinavia.

We arrived at Copenhagen about 8.30 on the following morning. When at Skagen I had written to Sir Ralph Paget, K.C.M.G., His Britannic Majesty's Minister to Denmark—whom we had known some years before when filling a similar position in Siam—telling him of our rescue. Lady Paget and he were waiting at the station to meet us. They straightway took my wife and myself off to the British Legation in Copenhagen, and insisted on us remaining there as their guests during our stay in the Danish capital. They were the personification of kindness to us, and helped us in every possible way, and it would be quite impossible for us to express adequately our great indebtedness to them. We obtained fresh *visés* for our passports from the British, Swedish, and Norwegian Consulates, and my wife, who had been unable in Siam to obtain a passport to travel to England, was granted an "emergency passport," on which she was described as an "ex-prisoner." The Germans had, quite unintentionally, it is true, helped her to get to England when our own Government had forbidden it.

We left Copenhagen on the evening of March 4th, and once more during the night embarked in a train ferry to cross to Sweden at Helsingborg. The next morning found us at Goteborg. The old Mauritius woman and her grandchild had been accommodated in a sleeping carriage with two berths. Not being used to such luxuries and not knowing what to do in such surroundings, they had deposited their garments on the bunks and slept on the floor, which doubtless came more natural to them!

The same evening we arrived at Christiania; unfortunately we saw nothing of this capital, as we arrived late at night, crossed to a hotel near the railway station, and returned to the station to resume our journey on the next morning before it was fully light. The whole of the next day we were travelling through Norway in brilliant dazzling sunshine, over snowclad mountains — some so high that vegetation was absent — finally leaving Bergen in the late afternoon of March 7th on the S.S. *Vulture*. From the *Wolf* to the *Vulture* did not look very promising!

Before leaving Norway every article of our baggage was carefully searched before being put on the boat. I asked the Customs officer what he was particularly looking for. "Bombs," he replied. But there were no German diplomats or members of German Legation staffs amongst us!

The ship was very full, so much so that many first-class passengers were compelled to travel third class, and among us were many people and officials of Allied nationality escaping from the disorders in Russia. We travelled full speed all night, and the passage was far from comfortable. Daybreak showed us the coast of the Shetlands — our first sight of the British Isles — and a few fussy armed trawlers shepherded us into the harbour of Lerwick, where we remained at anchor till dusk. We then set off again at full speed, and sighted the coast of Scotland in the morning. But it was not till past 2 p.m. that we arrived at Aberdeen. No sooner had the boat berthed in dock there than a representative of the Admiralty told us that all the *Igotz Mendi* prisoners were to proceed to London forthwith to be interrogated by the Admiralty. We had intended to have a few days' rest at Aberdeen after our strenuous travelling, but this was not allowed, so, much to our disgust and very much under protest, we spent still one more night out of bed, and so to London, where we arrived in a characteristic pea-soup fog on the morning of March 10th, after incessant travelling by train and sea for a week. We had not relished another sea voyage—and one across the North Sea least of all—but there was no help for it. We feared that as we had escaped the Germans once, they might make a special effort to sink us crossing the North Sea. But fortunately the U boats left us alone, though few, if any of us, turned in during those last few nights, for we felt we must still hold ourselves ready for any emergency. Arrived in London we were taken forthwith to the Admiralty, and there interrogated by the authorities as to the *Wolf's* exploits. Our adventures were really at an end at last.

At Skagen: German prizec rew of the" Igotz Mendi" under guard, awaiting internment.

With what joyful and thankful hearts did we reach home, once more to be united with our relatives and friends, who had long mourned us as dead. The shipping company had long ago abandoned all hope, the *Hitachi* had been posted missing at Lloyd's, letters of condolence had been received by our relatives, and we had the, even now in these exciting times, still unusual experience of reading our own obituary notices. We shall have to live up to them now! We heard from the Nippon Yushen Kaisha in London that the Japanese authorities had sent an expedition to look for the *Hitachi*. The expedition called at the Maldives, and had there found, in the atoll where we had first anchored in the *Wolf's* company, a door from the *Hitachi* splintered by shell-fire and a case of cocoanut identified as having been put on board the *Hitachi* at Colombo. The natives on this atoll could have told the expedition that at any rate the *Hitachi* was not sunk there, as they saw the *Wolf* and her prize sail away at different times. The *Hitachi's* disappearance was attributed to a submarine, though it was not explained how one managed to operate in the Indian Ocean!

We also heard in London that the Captain of the *Hitachi* committed suicide before the *Wolf* arrived in Germany.

No comment need be made on the German procedure of dragging their prisoners month after month over the oceans. Such a thing had never been done before. The Germans had had opportunities to release us, but had taken none to do so, as they had evidently determined not to allow any account of the *Wolf's* cruise to be made known. They might have put the *Hitachi* prisoners on the Maldives and left them there to get to Colombo as best they could, the Germans taking the ship; they might have sent the prisoners on the *Igotz Mendi* to Colombo or Java after they had taken what coal they wanted. As the Spanish Captain said, they had a right to take his contraband, but not his ship. But a question of right did not bother the Germans. Many times they promised him to release his ship, never intending to do so. Whenever they were asked why they did not release us when we thought it possible, they always advanced "military reasons" as the excuse. "That," as I said to the Captain, "covers a multitude of sins." The Commander of the *Wolf* had personally assured the married couples on the *Matunga* that they would be kept no longer than two months. But they were kept nearly seven. Some men had been kept prisoners on the *Wolf* for more than a year.

It was hard enough on the men, but infinitely worse for the women. One had been eight months, one seven, and others five months in captivity on the high seas, often under the worst possible conditions. But they all played their part well, and kept cheerful throughout, even when it appeared they were certain to be taken with their husbands into Germany.

Every man is liable to think, under such conditions, that he is in a worse case than his fellow-captives, and there were certainly examples of very hard luck amongst us. Mention of a few cases might be of interest. The American Captain had abandoned his sea calling for six years, and decided, at his wife's request, to make one more trip and take her to see her relatives in Newcastle, N.S.W. They never got there, but had eight months' captivity and landed in Denmark instead. Many sailors had left the Atlantic trade after encounters with the U boats in that ocean, only to be caught by the *Wolf* in the Pacific. One of the members of the Spanish crew had been a toreador, but his mother considered that calling too dangerous and recommended the sea as safer. Her son now thinks otherwise; perhaps she does too!

The Captain of a small sailing ship from Mauritius to West Australia, in ballast to load timber, saw the *Wolf* when a day off his destination. Not knowing her, he unwisely ran up the Red Ensign—a red rag to a bull, indeed—and asked the *Wolf* to report him "all well" at the next port. The *Wolf* turned about and sunk his little ship. Although the Captain was at one time on the *Wolf* almost in sight of his home in Mauritius, his next port was Kiel, where it is to be feared that he, an old man of seventy, was the reverse of "all well."

One of our fellow-prisoners had been on the P. & O. *Mongolia* when she was sunk by one of the *Wolf's* mines off Bombay. Later on, on the *Hitachi*, he was caught by the mine-layer herself! But he defeated the enemy after all, as he escaped on the *Igotz Mendi*! One of the seafaring men with us had already been torpedoed by the Huns in the Channel. Within a fortnight he was at sea again. The next time he was caught and his ship sunk by the *Wolf* off New Zealand. He also escaped on the *Igotz Mendi*, and when last seen ashore was dying to get to sea again, in a warm corner, so he said, so that he could "strafe the Huns" once more. They had held him prisoner for eight months, and he had some leeway to make up.

There was, too, the case of the Australians taken prisoner on the S.S. *Matunga*. The women and military doctors had certainly escaped on the *Igotz Mendi*, but there were taken into Germany from the *Matunga* three military officers and three elderly married civilians over military age. They were going but a week's voyage from their homes (July 1917); but, torn from their homes and families, they were to languish for months in a German internment camp. Neither must be forgotten the old captains and mates and young boys—some of the latter making their first sea voyage—taken into captivity in Germany, where they have probably been exhibited as illustrating the straits to which the war, and especially the U boat part of it, has reduced the glorious British mercantile marine. Our young men friends on the *Hitachi*, and the hundreds of prisoners, some of them captured more than a year before from British ships, were all taken into Germany, there to remain in captivity till the war was over.

I thought, until our timely rescue came, that our own case was a fairly hard one. I had retired from Government service in Siam, after spending twenty years there, and we had decided to spend some months at least, possibly "the duration," or even longer, in South Africa before proceeding home. It seemed hard lines that after twenty years in the Far East we were to come to Europe only to be imprisoned in Germany! We have escaped that, but our plans have gone hopelessly astray, for which I will *never* forgive the Huns, and our health has not improved by the treatment on our long voyage. But although we took six months to get from Siam to London, the Germans have succeeded in getting us home much earlier than we, or they, anticipated. I had been shipwrecked on my first voyage out to Siam in 1897, and on my last voyage home, twenty years after, had been taken prisoner and again shipwrecked! So my account was nicely balanced! But the culminating touch of escaping imprisonment in Germany by shipwreck was indeed wonderful!

Fortunately, one usually forgets the miseries of sea travel soon after one gets ashore. But never, I think, will one of us forget our long captivity at sea with our enemies; neither shall we forget the details of our capture and imprisonment, the dreary days and still drearier nights on the *Wolf* and *Igotz Mendi*, especially those spent in the icy north. Every detail of it all and of our wonderful escape at the last moment stands out so vividly in our memories.

And assuredly, not one of us will ever forget the canned crab, the bully beef, the beans, *and* the roll of the *Igotz Mendi*.

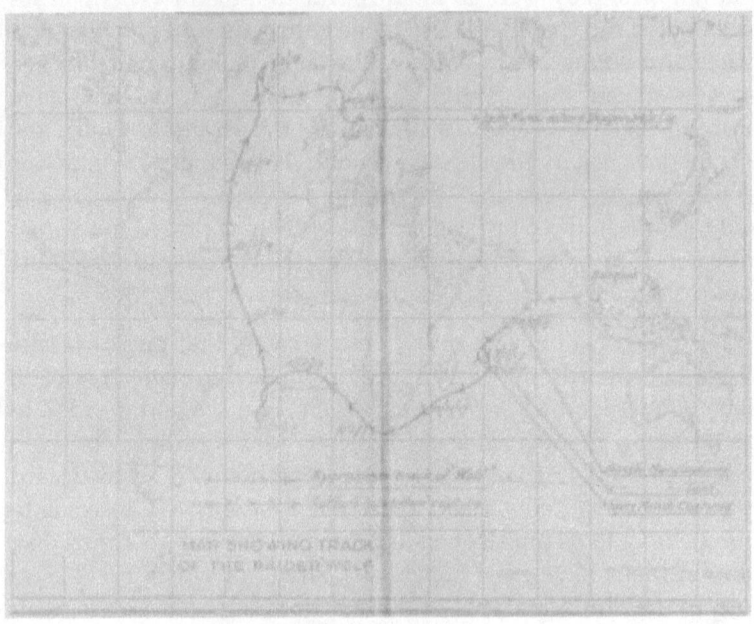

Map showing track oft her raider „Wolf"

www.ingramcontent.com/pod-product-compliance
Lightning Source LLC
Chambersburg PA
CBHW021624250426
43672CB00037B/2577